VENEERING MADE EASY
for School and Home Workshop

VENEERING
MADE EASY

for School and Home Workshop

By

HERMAN HJORTH

Revised by

ALBERT CONSTANTINE, JR.

ALBERT CONSTANTINE AND SON, INC.
2050 EASTCHESTER ROAD, BRONX, N. Y. 10461

Other Constantine Books

CONSTANTINE'S MANUAL FOR CRAFTSMEN

A standard reference book for craftsmen and home owners on woods, veneers, plywoods, tools, hardware, finishing materials, plans, books, etc. Lists and illustrates veneers, inlays and inserts in full color. Instructions on use of plywood, joints, etc. 126 pages, 10 in color.

CONSTANTINE'S WOOD-FINISHING MANUAL

How to finish and refinish furniture and other woodwork . . . use of professional type materials . . . staining, sealing, filling . . . high-lighting and glazing . . . blond and other modern finishes . . . finishing fir plywood . . . "tricks of the trade" used by professional finishers.

THE SECRETS OF MAKING INLAY PICTURES

A complete exposition of the art of making wood veneer pictures. It includes instructions for both the professional and amateur methods . . . how to cut the veneers expertly . . . assembling the picture . . . applying borders . . . gluing to panel . . . finishing . . . designing original pictures.

KNOW YOUR WOODS By Albert Constantine, Jr.

A useful, highly informative book on the fascinating world of woods. The complete, up-to-date guide on wood identification, characteristics, appearance, selection and usage. This authoritative book identifies 1,400 important woods. Includes over 500 revealing photographs and drawings. 384 pages.

CONSTANTINE'S HOME INSTRUCTION COURSES

COURSE IN WOOD FINISHING. A complete course in book form. Practical methods applied to everyday finishing problems of craftsman or home owner.

COURSE IN BETTER WOODWORKING. A concentrated course emphasizing the little-known, simple techniques that make the amateur a better woodworker.

INTRODUCTION

A KNOWLEDGE of veneering is invaluable to every woodworker, amateur or professional. It opens an entirely new field of accomplishment, because veneering makes it possible to construct finer furniture and other craftwork projects.

You may ask why this is so. Here are five reasons:

1. Face veneers cost only a fraction of the price of solid lumber of corresponding quality and appearance.

2. Veneers come in many rare woods and beautiful burls, mottles, crotches, stripes and other grain figures not available in solid stock.

3. Properly veneered panels do not shrink, expand or crack and are far stronger than corresponding solid wood.

4. Veneers are more uniform in color and grain and are perfectly smooth, therefore are much easier to finish well.

5. Expertly veneered projects have a more professional look and are correspondingly more valuable.

Thanks to the extraordinary modern glues now available, veneering is comparatively easy to do. All the basic principles are explained in detail in this book.

The reputation of Mr. Hjorth, the author, is preëminent in the United States as a teacher of woodwork. His various manuals, such as *Principles of Woodworking, Basic Woodworking Processes, Machine Woodworking, Operation of Common Woodworking Machines* and

Reproduction of Antique Furniture, are standard handbooks used almost universally in schools where woodworking is taught, as well as by amateur craftsmen everywhere.

Grateful acknowledgment is also made to the following for supplying illustrative material: The Metropolitan Museum of Art, American Walnut Manufacturer's Association, U. S. Forest Products Laboratories, United States Plywood Corporation, Penrod, Jurden & Clark Co., Bruce Publishing Co., Adjustable Clamp Co., Birdseye Veneer Co., George D. Emery Co.

No study of veneering would any longer be complete without emphasis on an unexpected new development which has taken place since the initial preparation of this text. The recent introduction of a new contact-type of adhesive, Veneer Glue, must be considered as a remarkably significant breakthrough in veneering technique. It could quite conceivably outdate, for many types of work, the long-established techniques requiring the use of clamps or presses. And it already has opened new frontiers in craftwork by making it now practicable to use enriching veneers where veneering could not be done before.

Because of its important role wherever veneering is studied or practiced, this latest advance in gluing veneers has been included in a special chapter, at the end of the book, in this revised edition.

Albert Constantine

TABLE OF CONTENTS

HISTORY OF VENEERING

THE original meaning of the word "veneer" was to embellish or decorate a surface with costlier and more beautiful materials such as wood, ivory, mother-of-pearl, tortoise shell, metals and even precious stones. It is in this manner that veneering was used in the earliest civilizations of which we have records: the Egyptian, Babylonian, Assyrian, Greek, and Roman.

In the tombs of the ancient kings of Egypt, pieces of furniture have been found, to which thin layers of wood have been glued more than 3500 years ago. But it is mainly from sculptured, painted and written records found by archæologists, where once stood Thebes, Babylon, Nineveh, Athens, Rome and other centers of these civilizations, that we have our knowledge of the ancient art of veneering. Like so many other arts, veneering and inlaying were lost during the dark Middle Ages. But with the Italian Renaissance (about 1500) came a return to the old Greek and Roman classicism modified by Byzantine and Oriental influences. Wood surfaces were again decorated mainly by "Intarsia," which is a form of inlaying resembling mosaic patterns. Woods of different color and shape are inserted into plain surfaces to form geometrical patterns, landscapes or other pictorial representations.

FIG. 1—Egyptian jewel box inlaid with ivory and wood

COURTESY OF THE METROPOLITAN MUSEUM OF ART

Marquetry, which came into use about 200 years later, differs from Intarsia in that the design, formed of varicolored veneers and other materials, is inlaid in a background of the same thickness forming a thin sheet, which is glued to solid wood.

During every succeeding art period, veneer and inlay were used in one form or another on all fine furniture. One of the most notable exponents of this art was the French master André Charles Boulle (1642—1732), who enjoyed the patronage of Louis XIV

The art of cutting and matching veneers, so that the natural figure of the wood forms patterns of rare beauty, was first discovered and utilized during the Eighteenth Century (Fig. 2) This method of veneering, which is the one in vogue today, was employed

FIG. 2—Veneered highboy, American, 1725-1750

extensively by the great English cabinet makers Chippendale, Hepplewhite and Sheraton, and also by our own famous Duncan Phyfe and his contemporaries. The phase of the Colonial Period, which was known as the American Empire and characterized both by excellent designs and craftsmanship, ended about 1830.

During the latter half of the Nineteenth Century, it seems as if all forms of artistic expressions declined and died everywhere. In this country this period is sometimes referred to as "the dark ages of black walnut" because of the conspicuous lack of artistic production of any kind and because black walnut was used extensively for the atrocious furniture produced.

The gingerbread decorations of black walnut were later superseded by the golden oak mission monstrosities. Practically no veneer was used during this time because of the mistaken public notion that the wood should be "solid."

ADVANTAGES OF VENEERING

THE penchant for solid wood has caused an odium to be attached to veneered work. Even to this day some people consider veneered work as not quite genuine, as something that will wear off or tarnish like plated metal, while the fact is that modern veneered furniture is practically the only kind that will not warp, crack or fall to pieces in present-day steam-heated homes.

STRUCTURAL FEATURES. As described more fully in the next chapter, a piece of veneer is a very thin sheet of wood, usually about 1/28" in thickness. One sheet is a "single-ply veneer." When several sheets or plies are glued together at right angles to each other we have what is called plywood. A plywood board is many times stronger than solid wood of the same thickness, and less likely to be split by nails driven into it, or broken under blows or stress. Hence, plywood construction may be made thinner than solid construction with consequent economy in material. The natural tendency of wood to absorb or give off moisture, according to the varying moisture content of the air (see Chapter VI), is largely eliminated in plywood construction, because the tendency of any layer to contract or expand is offset or defeated by other layers glued at right angles to it.

Although this scientific way of utilizing veneer was not developed until the beginning of the present century, the plywood industry is now a large and important one. In the furniture industry this scientific knowledge of veneering combined with its older, decorative values has enabled the manufacturer to create a product that is greatly superior to solid wood, both structurally and artistically.

As a matter of fact, it would be impossible to construct a piece of furniture of such highly figured wood as, for example, burl walnut, because the grain of such wood is produced by disease or accident, is structurally weak and would split and warp all out of shape. Other woods, particularly tropical varieties as ebony, are so dense, that if a piece of furniture were constructed from the solid wood, it would be so heavy as to be practically immovable. Moreover, the combination of such pieces of solid wood into patterns similar to those obtainable with veneer would be a physical impossibility.

It therefore stands to reason that straight-grained lumber must be used for strength and highly figured wood for decoration. This combination is only possible in veneered work, where the core or inside part is made of plywood or a straight-grained and not too heavy wood. To further prevent warping, a solid wood core is glued together of narrow strips. The core is veneered with straight-grained wood on both sides and at right angles to the grain (Fig. 3). These veneers, which are plain and inexpensive are called crossbands, because they are glued at right angles or across the core, thereby binding it more closely together. The face veneer, usually selected from rare and costly woods, is then glued to the outside surface and a plainer veneer to the back or inside surface. The grain of these veneers runs in the same direction as that of the core and at right angles to the crossbands. (See also Chapters VI and VII).

This construction is not necessarily cheap. In the finest type of mahogany furniture produced, both core and crossbands are made of straight-grained mahogany. While this costs considerably less than

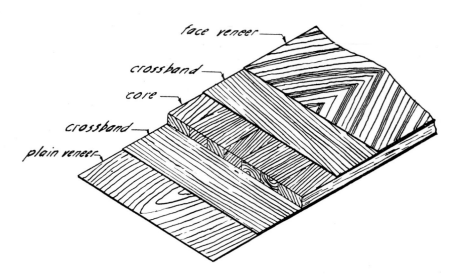

FIG. 3—Core, crossbands, face and back veneers

12

highly figured mahogany, the labor costs of producing the veneered construction offset the saving effected in the purchase of wood.

On the other hand, cores that are just as good and strong may be made of much cheaper kinds of wood or even of wood unsuitable for other purposes on account of blemishes, worm holes or other defects. In such cases a considerable saving may be effected, especially by home craftsmen or students who need not take labor costs into consideration.

METHODS OF PRODUCING VENEERS

MOST face veneers used on fine furniture are cut from tropical woods. Anyone who has visited the tropics, whether in this hemisphere or the Eastern, readily understands the well-nigh insurmountable difficulties of felling and transporting huge and exceedingly heavy trees growing in a dense tropical forest. The inaccessibility of the forests, the lack of transportation facilities, the problem of primitive labor, the constant danger from wild and poisonous animals and the threat to health from tropical diseases are just a few of these.

Once the tree is felled, the branches are removed and the trunk cut into lengths. Sometimes these are roughly squared (Fig. 4) and sometimes left in the round. They are then floated down rivers or streams or dragged by oxen or man power over land to the coast, where they are loaded on steamers and transported to sawmills often thousands of miles distant. Arrived at the sawmill, the logs are

FIG. 4—"Squaring" mahogany logs in the bush. The man at the left with the two "machetes' is beating the time, and the men on opposite sides of the log are supposed to work in unison

Fig. 5.—Opening up an African mahogany log

dumped overboard into a logpond, where they are usually kept floating until wanted at the mill. Immersion in the water protects the logs from insect and fungi attacks and prevents rotting and splitting.

African mahogany logs measuring as much as six feet after squaring, and weighing from ten to fifteen tons, are sometimes handled by large sawmills.

SAWING THE LOG.—Hoisted from the pond into the mill, the log is mounted on a car resembling a flat railroad car, which runs on a track. The sawyer controls the powerful machinery which moves the log to the carriage as well as the carriage itself. This is now moved slowly against a large band-saw having wheels eight feet or more in diameter and a blade as much as fifty feet long and fourteen inches wide.

The first cut is generally made near the center of the log for the purpose of "opening" it and examining the wood of the interior (Fig. 5). Only a small percentage of the logs have a highly figured

FIG. 6—Sawing veneers

16

FIG. 7—Rotary veneer cutting. One log is in the lathe and another ready for cutting. Three log centers are in the foreground

FIG. 8—Slicing
rosewood veneers

grain suitable for veneers. Those having straight, ordinary grain are sawn up into boards, those having the rare, figured grain are sawn into "flitches," which are smaller timbers squared on all four sides. Their thickness, width, and length depend upon the size of the log and the extent of the figured grain.

There are four generally accepted methods of cutting veneer. These are: sawing, slicing, rotary cutting, and half rounding.

Sawed veneers are cut from flitches mounted on a movable carriage. The type of saw used is generally the segmental circular saw, the blade of which is built up of many parts or segments bolted to a cast-iron hub (Fig. 6). Although these segments are very thin, the saw wastes as much lumber as it cuts when sawing veneers of the standard 1/28″ in thickness. Thicker veneers may also be sawed, in which case the waste, of course, is proportionately less.

Sliced veneers are cut with a knife. In this case the flitch must first be softened by steaming or cooking in boiling water for several hours. The veneer slicer is a very heavy machine consisting of two main parts, a movable bed to which the flitch is bolted, and a knife supported in a rigid frame. The bed moves up and down while the knife remains stationary (Fig. 8).

FIG. 9—A huge temperature-controlled mechanical veneer dryer of modern type

19

By means of diagonal guide bars the veneer is sliced with a shearing cut as it moves against the knife. After each cut the knife is given a slight sideways movement, corresponding to the thickness of the veneer cut, so that all the sheets are exactly of the same thickness, the standard being 1/28″.

As in sawed veneer, the sheets are numbered and piled in the order in which they are cut. All the sheets cut from a flitch are always kept together because only veneer cut from the same log can be matched.

Rotary cut veneers are also cut with a knife, but from a whole, round log instead of a flitch. Being cut with a knife, the log must first be softened by steaming or boiling. The bark is cut off, then the log is mounted in a lathe and rotated against a knife which is held rigidly. By giving the knife a slight sideways movement in the direction of the center of the log a continuous sheet or peeling of uniform thickness results. This is again cut into suitable widths on a clipper machine. The center of the log is cut up for crating lumber (Fig. 7).

Rotary cut veneers are more economical to produce than either sawed or sliced veneers. The figure of the wood is therefore not the main consideration, but rather the quantity of the output. Thicknesses of rotary cut veneers vary according to the purpose for which they are to be used. They are used mainly in the manufacture of doors, plywood and crossbandings and are cut chiefly from birch, gum, oak, poplar and Douglas fir.

Half Rounded veneers are also cut on a lathe. In this case half the log is bolted to the lathe and revolved against the knife. The sheets of veneer cut in this manner are slightly rounded. Walnut stumps and bird's-eye maple are often cut in this way.

DRYING VENEERS.—All types of veneers are dried after they are cut. This is done in various ways. Formerly the veneer was placed in racks, but now immense machine driers speed the work (Fig. 9).

Another method is to pass the sheets through a series of steam-heated rollers.

...till another method is the platen dryer, which consists of a series of heated plates moving up and down like bellows alternately squeezing and releasing the sheets of veneer placed between them.

After drying, the veneers cut from the same flitch are placed in numerical sequence, measured, and piled in bundles.

HOW A TREE PRODUCES THE LUMBER WE USE

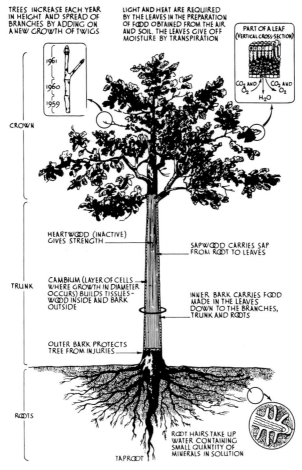

TREES INCREASE EACH YEAR IN HEIGHT AND SPREAD OF BRANCHES BY ADDING ON A NEW GROWTH OF TWIGS

LIGHT AND HEAT ARE REQUIRED BY THE LEAVES IN THE PREPARATION OF FOOD OBTAINED FROM THE AIR AND SOIL. THE LEAVES GIVE OFF MOISTURE BY TRANSPIRATION

PART OF A LEAF (VERTICAL CROSS-SECTION)

CO_2 AND O_2 CO_2 AND O_2
H_2O

1961
1960
1959

CROWN

HEARTWOOD (INACTIVE) GIVES STRENGTH

SAPWOOD CARRIES SAP FROM ROOT TO LEAVES

CAMBIUM (LAYER OF CELLS WHERE GROWTH IN DIAMETER OCCURS) BUILDS TISSUES— WOOD INSIDE AND BARK OUTSIDE

TRUNK

INNER BARK CARRIES FOOD MADE IN THE LEAVES DOWN TO THE BRANCHES, TRUNK AND ROOTS

OUTER BARK PROTECTS TREE FROM INJURIES

ROOTS

ROOT HAIRS TAKE UP WATER CONTAINING SMALL QUANTITY OF MINERALS IN SOLUTION

TAPROOT

THE SHOOT TIPS, ROOT TIPS AND CAMBIAL LAYER ARE THE GROWING PARTS. THE TREE TAKES IN OXYGEN OVER ITS ENTIRE SURFACE THROUGH PORES ON LEAVES, TWIGS, BRANCHES, TRUNK AND ROOTS

Courtesy of
U.S. Dept. of Agriculture

21

TYPES OF VENEERS

VENEERS used in cabinet making fall into three classes: cross-banding, plain unfigured veneers, and face veneers.

The *Crossbanding or Crossbands* as shown in Fig. 3 are veneers that are glued to both sides of the core or inside part of a veneered panel. They are called crossbands, because they are glued at right angles to the grain of the core or across it, and thus bind or hold it firmly together and prevent it from warping.

Crossbanding is both sliced and rotary cut. That cut by the slicing method is considered the finest, because it has a straighter grain and is flatter and easier to handle. Different woods may be used for this purpose, but poplar and Honduras mahogany are considered the best, because both woods hold glue well, do not tear easily and do not curl. Rotary cut poplar veneer, 1/20", is the most common and most widely used crossbanding veneer. Crossbanding may be obtained in many thicknesses as 1/16" and 1/20". The standard thickness of sliced crossbanding is 1/28".

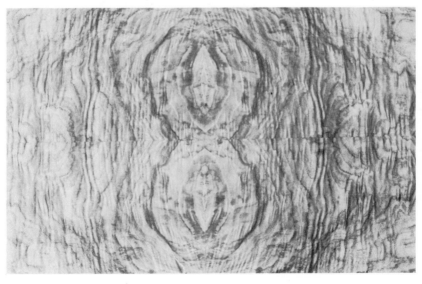

FIG. 10—Four-piece match of stump walnut veneer

22

The price of mahogany crossbanding is about 50% over that of poplar.

Plain unfigured veneers are used on the side that is not visible, such as the underside of table tops. These veneers, which are also called back-veneers, are glued at right angles to the crossbanding.

From a structural point of view it is very important that both surfaces are veneered alike, as this tends to prevent warping.

Face Veneers are usually sawed or sliced, although some, like bird's-eye maple, are rotary cut or half rounded. Face veneers are selected according to grain, markings, texture and color. The standard thickness is 1/28″.

Grain in wood varies from the plain, regular lines to the irregular, intricate lines running here and there in a wayward irresponsible manner.

FIG. 11—Typical walnut crotch veneer

Markings are intricate figures in wood that cannot be classified as grain. Veneers of the burl, stump, or crotch variety have exceptional figurings, caused by distortion from normal growth, which is explained as follows:

BUTT OR STUMP VENEERS

At the junction of the larger roots with the stem of a tree and to a less extent where the branches join the stem, the fibres are considerably distorted, producing various kinds of cross figures, particularly mottle and curly grain. Veneers cut from such portions of the tree are highly figured. (See Fig. 10.)

CROTCH

At forks in the tree trunk or where large branches join the trunk, the fibres run in different directions in closely adjoining portions, often giving lumber cut from such parts of a tree a pattern resembling a cluster of plumes (see Fig. 11). This is called "crotch figure," or, more often, "crotch mahogany," "crotch walnut," etc., according to the kind of wood.

BURLS

Burls are large wart-like growths on tree trunks. They contain the dark piths of a large number of buds. The formation of these buds, which rarely develop, apparently is due to some injury sustained by the tree. Throughout the burl the fibres are very irregularly contorted so that the grain cannot be said to run in any particular direction. Burls may occur on almost any species, but walnut, ash, cherry, and redwood burls are among the most highly prized in furniture woods. Fig. 12 shows burl in walnut.

Figures in wood, both grain and markings, are known under different names. Typical mahogany figures are: straight stripe, broken stripe or mottle, blister, fiddleback and crotch (Figs. 13, 14, 15, 16).

By texture is understood the play of light and shadow on figured wood. If looked at from one angle certain parts appear light

FIG. 12—Four-piece match of walnut burl veneer

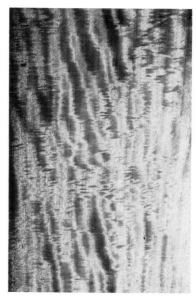

Fig. 13—Mahogany mottled and striped

Fig. 14—Mahogany. Broken stripe and raindrop

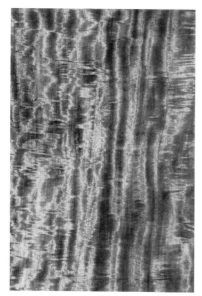

Fig. 15—Mahogany. Mottle stripe

Fig. 16.—Mahogany-Crotch horsetail figure

and others dark. If looked at from another angle, it will be seen that the dark parts are now light and the light parts dark. Color is a very important consideration in selecting and combining veneers. Different species of wood vary a great deal in color. Tropical woods are particularly rich in color. See list following.

A great many different kinds of veneers are manufactured; some are very rare and correspondingly expensive, others are more plentiful and can be had at a very reasonable figure. Obviously the beginner in the art of veneering should not use the rarer kinds until some experience and facility in handling veneers have been obtained. This is good advice not only on account of the price, but also because the highly figured veneers are usually very brittle and curly and therefore harder to manipulate. The following veneers, with one or two exceptions, are moderately priced and suitable for the simpler forms of veneering explained in detail in the succeeding chapters.

Mahogany is the cabinet wood par excellence, because of the inherent beauty of the wood and its comparative freedom from warping and shrinkage.

It is a tropical wood, the principal supply coming from West Africa, Central and South America, and the West Indies. West Indian or "Spanish mahogany" is the finest, being close grained, fairly hard and of a rich, reddish brown color and beautiful figure. American mahogany, known to the trade as "Mexican mahogany," is not as hard or close grained as Spanish mahogany, nor of such rich color. Most of this wood is straight grained. African mahogany trees grow to a very large size. Logs weighing as much as fifteen tons have been received at American sawmills. The wood is both of a rich color and beautiful figure. Ninety per cent of manufactured mahogany lumber and veneers are produced from African logs. Because the supply is rather plentiful, veneers cost only from 15 cents to 48 cents per sq. ft.

Crotch mahogany is one of the rarer and most richly figured types of veneer. It is more difficult to handle and also more expensive, varying in price from 48 cents to 50 cents per sq. ft.

Black Walnut is a North American tree growing practically everywhere in the United States, but most plentifully in the Middle West.

26

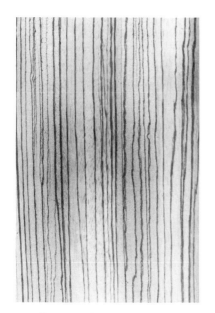

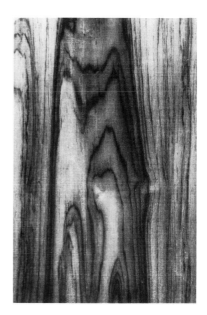

FIG. 17—Zebrawood veneer

FIG. 18—Rosewood veneer

FIG. 19—Bird's-eye maple veneer

FIG. 20—Sliced red gum veneer

27

Walnut veneer is available in the following figures: plain striped, wavy and mottle. The latter is a highly figured veneer of unusual beauty. Black walnut varies in color from light to dark brown with occasional dark irregular streaks. The price varies from 20 cents to 65 cents per sq. ft.

Vermilion or Padouk is a hard, strong wood of a rich red (oxblood) color. It varies in price from 27 cents to 35 cents per sq. ft.

Oriental Wood somewhat resembles American Walnut and is often used in its place. It varies in price from 18 cents to 22 cents per sq. ft.

Zebrawood is a light colored wood with a very pronounced stripe costing about 25 cents per sq. ft. (Fig. 17.)

East Indian Rosewood is a wood with a very pronounced dark purple stripe. It is priced from 22 cents to 28 cents per sq. ft. (Fig. 18.)

Satinwood is of a rich golden color, often with a figure of rare beauty (Fig. 47). It is used in combination with other woods, especially mahogany. Figured satinwood is rather expensive, varying in price from 30 cents to 38 cents per sq. ft.

By *Foreign Walnut* is understood Circassian, English, French, Italian and Turkish walnut. All these species are very similar. They are of a lighter color than the domestic walnut and have a fine, close texture. Circassion walnut has a very intricate figure with characteristic dark markings.

Maple is available in three figures: Bird's-eye, Curly, and Blister. It is usually rotary cut or half rounded and costs from 22 cents to 40 cents per sq. ft. (Fig. 19.)

Red Gum veneer is sliced on the quarter. It is generally 1/20 of an inch thick. It varies in price from 15 cents to 18 cents per sq. ft. (Fig. 20.)

Birch is a hard and strong wood growing in the Northern part of the United States. It is used extensively in furniture construction, in interior woodworking, in the manufacture of plywood and in laminated chair seat construction. There are several varieties of birch, as yellow, red, and white birch. Birch veneer is both sliced and rotary cut. It sometimes has a very beautiful figure. Birch veneer is inexpensive.

USE OF VENEERS IN FURNITURE CONSTRUCTION.—Veneers are used in practically all types of furniture construction, both expensive and moderately priced. It follows that the most beautiful veneers are used on the parts of a piece of furniture where they will show to the best advantage, as on table tops and drawer fronts. Crotch mahogany and burl walnut are typical veneers selected for this purpose. These veneers are cut and matched to form beautiful patterns which are often further enriched by borders and inlays of contrasting, rich colored woods such as zebrawood, East Indian rosewood, or satinwood.

Veneers are also used for side panels, backs, bottoms, drawer bottoms and dust panels between drawers. Plainer and less expensive veneers are used for these parts.

CHECK LIST OF AVAILABLE VENEERS. For the ready identification of all those veneers that can be purchased in either small or large quantities, Albert Constantine and Son, Inc., which has made a specialty of veneer logs and veneers since 1812, has developed a standard list of veneers in which each is given an identifying number.

This list has many uses. For example, the master drawings of the entire line of Constantine inlaid pictures carry numbers that immediately identify the veneers used for each part. *Constantine's Manual for Craftsmen* also has a large chart printed in full color which shows the actual appearance of all the standard veneers—and here again the numbers are used to identify them.

Since it is interesting to know the relative cost of the various veneers, the prices current when this book was published have been added. These prices represent the retail cost of the veneers when purchased in small quantities. In quantities of more than 100 square feet of any one veneer, the price naturally would be somewhat less. While these prices change from time to time, they will serve to give an approximate idea of how much the various veneers cost in relation to each other — which veneers are relatively inexpensive and which, because of rarity, unusual figuration or other reasons, are most costly.

STANDARD VENEER LIST

WITH IDENTIFYING NUMBERS AND
APPROXIMATE PRICES

No.	Veneer	Price per sq. ft.
1	AMBOYNA BURLS (Amboyna)	$ .90
1A	ASH (USA)	.20
2	ASPEN (USA) crotches	.38
3	" stripe	.17
4	" mottle figure	.30
5	AVODIRE (Africa) plain	.18
6	" stripe	.25
7	" mottle	.30
8	BEECH (USA)	.20
8A	BELLAROSE (Australia)	.19
9	BENIN (Africa) stripe	.25
11	BLACKWOOD (Australia)	.17
12	*BOXWOOD (West Indies) sawed $\frac{1}{24}''$	.40
14	BUBINGA (Africa) stripe and mottle figure	.30
15	BUTTERNUT (USA)	.25
15A	CANALETTA (South America)	.22
16	CARPATHIAN ELM BURLS (France)	.43
17A	CEDAR AROMATIC RED, sawed $\frac{1}{20}''$	.23
19	CHERRY (USA) plain	.18
20	" figured	.28
21	COCOBOLA (Nicaragua)	.35
22	DAO (Australia)	.25
23	EBONY, Maccassar (India) known as golden ebony, sawed, $\frac{1}{24}''$	.60
24	EBONY, Maccassar (India) sliced $\frac{1}{28}''$	.50
25	*EBONY, Gaboon (Africa) entirely black, $\frac{1}{24}''$ sawed	1.25

* Widths 3½" to 5"

No.	Veneer	Price per sq. ft.
26	FLORESA (Central America)	$ .25
26A	GUMWOOD (USA) quartered sliced	.18
26B	GONCALO ALVES (Brazil)	.35
27	HAREWOOD (England) dyed grey in England	.40
28	HAREWOOD (England) extra choice	.55
29	HOLLY (USA)	.30
29A	IMBUYA (Brazil)	.20
29B	IROKA (Africa) figured	.25
30	*KINGWOOD (Brazil) sawed $\frac{1}{24}$"	.60
31	KELOBRA (Mexico) straight stripe	.25
34	LACEWOOD (Australia) also known as salana, and silky Oak, in either small or large size figure	.40
35A	LIMBA (Africa)	.25
36	MACCA WOOD (South America)	.20
37	MADRONE BURL (USA) known also as Manchurian maple	.55
38	MAHOGANY (Africa) plain	.15
39	" straight stripe	.22
40	" mottle	.30
41	" crotches	.75
42	MAHOGANY (Mexico) plain	.18
43	" mottle	.27
44	MAHOGANY (Cuba)	.27
46	MAIDOU (East Indies) long wood	.60
47	" burls	.90
48	MAPLE (USA) quartered sliced	.25
49	" curly	.30
50	" bird's eye	.30
52	" burl	.50
53	MARNUT (Brazil)	.25

* Widths 3½" to 5"

No.	Veneer	Price per sq. ft.
54	MYRTLE (USA) burls and swirls	.50
55	NARRA STRIPE	.28
56	OAK (USA) sliced rift $\frac{1}{28}''$	.25
56c	" sliced qtd. figure $\frac{1}{28}''$	.25
57	OAK (England) sliced $\frac{1}{20}''$	.35
58	OKUME (Africa)	.20
59	ORIENTAL Wood stripe	.18
60	ORIENTAL Wood mottle	.22
61	PADOUK (India) known also as vermilion; straight stripe	.27
62	PADOUK (India) small mottle figure	.38
63	PALDAO (Australia)	.26
63A	PLATINA (Philippines)	.25
64	PEARWOOD (European)	.30
65	PEROBA (South America)	.30
66	PIQUA (Africa) also known as Bosse, very beautiful light tan colored wood; figured	.27
67	PURPLEHEART (Dutch Guiana) also called Amaranth	.35
68	PRIMA VERA (Central America) commonly known as White Mahogany; stripe	.25
69	PRIMA VERA—mottle figure	.30
70	ROSEWOOD (Brazil) straight stripe	.50
71	" leaf figure	.50
72	ROSEWOOD (East Indies) straight stripe	.50
74	ROSEWOOD (Honduras) leaf figure	.23
75	REDWOOD BURLS (California)	.65
76	SATINWOOD (Ceylon) straight stripe	.35
77	" mottle and bee's wing	.42

		Price per sq. ft.
No.	Veneer	
78	SATINWOOD (West Indies) used by marquetry manufacturers	.40
78A	SINORO (Philippines)	.22
79	SNAKEWOOD (Surinam) sawed $\frac{1}{24}$"	.60
80	SEPELE (Africa) very fine stripe	.25
81	SYCAMORE (England) fine figure	.35
81A	SYCAMORE (USA)	.25
82	TAMO (Japan) leaf figure	.28
83	" peanut figure	.45
84	TEAK (India) plain stripe	.38
85	" figured	.38
86	THUYA (Africa) in burl figure only	.75
87	*TULIPWOOD (Brazil) sliced $\frac{1}{28}$"	.40
88	TULIPWOOD (Mexico)	.27
91	WALNUT (USA) straight quartered stripe plain	.25
92	WALNUT (USA) straight quartered stripe figured	.40
93	WALNUT (USA) plain leaf figure	.22
94	" butts	.40
95	" crotches	.50
96	" burls	.75
97	WALNUT CIRCASSIAN (Russia) leaf figure	.25
98	WALNUT (France) straight stripe	.35
99	" leaf figure	.30
100	YUBA (Australia) mottle figure	.38
101	ZEBRA WOOD (Africa) also known as Zebrano straight stripe	.30

* Widths 3½" to 5"

33

No.	Veneer			Price per sq. ft.
102	CROSSBANDING (whitewood or poplar)		$\frac{1}{28}''$	.11
103	"	"	$\frac{1}{20}''$	.13
104	"	"	$\frac{1}{8}''$	.20

COLORED 1/28". 120 Gulf Stream Green,
121 Emerald Green, 122 Olive Green,
123 Tropic Green, 124 Deep Purple,
125 Tangerine, 126 Canary Yellow, } .35
127 Flamingo Pink, 128 Pastel Pink,
129 Royal Blue, 130 Sunset Red,
131 Jet Black

HANDLING AND STORING VENEERS IN THE SHOP

How to Store Veneer. To prevent buckling of veneer sheets on hand, lay the sheets flat on a perfectly flat surface such as a table, a wide shelf or a piece of plywood. Keep the edges and ends as even as possible. Place a flat board or panel on top of the pile and weight it down evenly all over. Storage of veneers in the average basement which is both cool and somewhat damp is preferable to the furnace room or hot attic.

How to Straighten Buckled Veneer. A day or two before you will be ready to use the veneer, sprinkle each buckled sheet very lightly with water. The best way to prevent over-wetting is to dip a whiskbroom in a pail of water and flip the water on the veneer. One or two flips of the wrist will sprinkle all the water you should apply. Lay the moistened sheets on a flat surface. Sandwich newspaper between veneer sheets. Place a flat panel on top. Add heavy, even weights to the panel. The more weight, the better. Leave the veneers in this form for 24 hours or more, and remove only when ready to use them.

Veneer should never be moistened just before use. Unless veneer is dry when glue is applied it is apt to shrink excessively and cause splits or blisters in the finished panel. This is one of the most important rules in veneering.

GLUE
HISTORY - COMPOSITION - PREPARATION - USE

B ECAUSE no panel and no glue joint is better than the glue used, the selection of the proper glue is of the utmost importance. The factors of strength, convenience in handling and adaptability to work in hand warrant careful study. There are several types of glue available, of which the following are commonly used for veneering in home workshops, school shops and woodworking shops in general.

UREA RESIN GLUES

Urea resin glue is the most widely used type of glue for commercial production of veneered panels because of its light color, the fact that it does not stain, its high strength and water resistance and its fast cure at room temperature or in the hot press. These same qualities make it a preferred glue for home and school use.

CASCAMITE, a urea resin glue made by the Chemical Division of the Borden Company, is an adhesive of this type and will be used as an example throughout this discussion. Another well-known urea resin glue is Weldwood.

In commercial use, urea resin is generally supplied in liquid form and mixed with catalyst, filler and flour-and-water extender. The storage life of liquid resin is, however, limited to a few months. For home, school and small-shop use, the glue is supplied in powder form with filler and catalyst incorporated. In this form, the storage life is at least one year when the container is kept tightly closed and stored in a cool, dry place. The powder glue need only be mixed with water in the proper proportions and is then ready for use.

If in doubt as to the age of urea resin glue, see if the powder goes into smooth solution. If it does, it will make a full-strengh bond. If the powder is lumpy and does not go into solution, but feels grainy or sandy between the fingers, it is overage, partially insoluble and should be discarded.

For best results with urea resin glue, the wood, glue and curing temperature should be at least 70° F. At lower curing temperature, full strength is not attained — even though the bond is heated later on. The wood, particularly the solid wood or the cores used for veneered panels, should have a moisture content of at least 6 percent. This can be attained by storing the wood where there is a normal humidity in the air. There should also be adequate facilities for applying even and high pressure over the entire gluing surface so that wood surfaces are brought into intimate contact and thick glue lines are avoided.

When mixed, the liquid glue mix has a usable life of 5 to 7 hours at 70° F. At the end of its life the thickened glue should not be diluted, but thrown away and a fresh mix made if required.

When the glue is applied to the wood, an assembly time of 10 to 15 minutes may be taken before pressure is applied. Higher temperatures may shorten this assembly period. In any case, the glue film should be wet or tacky to the touch when pressure is applied.

Pressure Periods at 70° F.
High density woods: 5 to 7 hours
Low density woods: 4 to 6 hours

NOTE: The question of how to reduce the pressure time becomes of great interest to all who progress beyond elementary veneering and wish to turn out work in larger quantity for commercial purposes. Fortunately, urea resins are highly sensitive to heat. The curing time can be reduced from four hours at 70° F. to *four minutes* at 200° F. Where this extra speed is required, so-called Uskon electrically-heated rubber blankets, steam-heated platens or other heating methods may be used. The Uskon blankets, which are especially convenient, are made by the Washburn Electric Co., 202 Sherwood Place, Englewood, N. J. When heat is used to speed the curing time, the finished bond will withstand exposures to high humidity or even cycles of actual water soaking. It is stainfree and relatively permanent for any interior use. Test panels now over 15 years old show practically no deterioration of the bond under normal interior conditions.

CASEIN GLUE

Dry powder casein glues (CASCO GRADE A) have largely been replaced by urea resins for veneering. They are, however, recommended under the following conditions: When gluing conditions are colder than 70° F.; when surfaces are rough or uneven or good pressure is lacking so that there is bound to be a thick glue film; when gluing dense decorative laminates such as Formica and Micarta; when the finished bond will be subjected to high temperature such as counter tops to hold hot dishes, radiator covers, boxes to hold lights, and the like. Casein glues are alkaline and will cause stain when used with acid woods such as oak, mahogany, etc.

Like urea resin glues, casein glues are supplied as a dry powder to be mixed with water at the time of use. A smooth, creamy solution should result. (Grainy or sandy mixtures that do not smooth out on standing for 15 to 30 minutes indicate an overage powder that has become insoluble and should be discarded.)

Gluing temperature, moisture content of the wood and amount of pressure are not so critical with casein glue as with urea resins, but for best results with any type of glue, accurate fitting, normal moisture content and fairly high pressures are preferred.

The usable life, assembly time and pressure periods for casein glues are approximately the same as for urea resins — at the same temperatures. Under cold gluing conditions, all these time factors are greatly increased. Though not as water-resistant as urea resin glues, casein glues will withstand practically any interior moisture condition as shown by 40 to 50 years' experience with this type of glue.

This glue is now available only in large drums for commercial users. For other users, Elmer's Glue-All is recommended.

POLYVINYL RESIN GLUE

This new type of resin glue (ELMER'S GLUE-ALL) has become widely popular because of its convenience. It is supplied in liquid form, ready for use. No mixing is required, and the glue remains in good condition when stored at room temperature in a tightly closed container. (Polyvinyl resins are acidic and should not be kept in metal containers or where the vapors come in contact with metal:

Contact with metal causes glue stain — and corrosion of the metal surfaces.)

Polyvinyls should not be used when the glue, wood or room are colder than 60° F. At lower temperatures, the glue turns a chalky white and the strength is affected. At 60° or higher, the glue film becomes transparent and stainfree.

Polyvinyl resins cure very quickly — in 20 to 30 minutes at 70° F. (Assembly time is, therefore, much shorter, and the surfaces must be spread, assembled and put under pressure within four or five minutes so that the film does not dry before pressure is applied.)

Polyvinyl resins are not as water-resistant as urea resin or casein glues. They are also slightly thermoplastic and tend to "creep" in bonds under high tensile strain and subjected to temperatures over 160° to 180° F.

RESORCIN RESIN GLUES

Room-temperature-setting resin glues (ELMER'S WATERPROOF GLUE) are recommended for all gluing where the finished construction is to be exposed to the weather or continuous water soaking or continued cycles of soaking and drying — such as boats, toys, outdoor, furniture, sports equipment, etc. (This is the only type of glue which complies with Military Specifications for wood constructions for marine use.)

The glue is supplied as a liquid resin with a separate container of powder catalyst. The resin and catalyst are mixed in weighed proportions at time of use.

Like urea resin glues, the wood, glue and curing temperature must be 70° F. or higher when resorcins are used. At lower curing temperatures, full strength and water-resistance are not developed.

Resorcin resins are a dark wine color and will darken further on exposure to light. When used for veneering light-colored wood, every precaution must be taken to prevent excess penetration into the veneers where it may bleed through and show on the face side.

Usable life of the mixed glue, assembly time and curing temperatures are approximately the same as for urea resins. Resorcins are also highly heat sensitive and cure very quickly when the glue-line temperature can be raised.

OTHER ADHESIVES

Various other glues are used in industrial veneering, but do not need to be considered here. However, there are several more glues available to amateurs which should be mentioned for completeness.

One, of course, is the old-time stand-by of all cabinetmakers — animal glue, or hide glue as it is often called. This is a difficult glue to use because it requires the workroom to be very warm, the wood and veneer must be warm, and heated metal plates and caul boards are required; besides, the utmost speed is necessary in spreading the glue and closing and clamping the joints.

Animal or hide glue is made from hoofs, bones, sinews and skin linings of cattle. This glue is manufactured in many different grades of varying strength which are difficult for the layman to distinguish. The best grades are strong and dependable. Animal glue is made in hard sheets or cakes, which must be broken and soaked overnight in water. It is then heated in a double boiler to a temperature which must not exceed 150 degrees F. Repeated heating weakens the glue and makes it too thick. It must then be thinned with water, which further weakens it. For the best results it is important that animal glue is freshly made and of the right consistency and temperature. Gluing must be done quickly and in a warm room so as not to chill the glue before clamps can be applied.

Liquid hide glue is a convenient preparation of animal glue in ready-to-use form. It has many of the same qualities as hot glue, but is slow setting so that there is ample time to coat and assemble the work before applying pressure. The temperature of the workroom, wood and cauls does not need to be so high, but should be above 60°.

Liquid fish glue also sets slowly. It is rarely used for veneering except in patching or making small projects to which veneer is applied after assembly. If the glue is too thick to spread readily, the glue container may be placed in a dish of hot water or otherwise warmed to a moderate degree. A better joint will result if, after the glue has been spread, an interval of about five minutes is allowed to elapse before laying the veneer and applying pressure. Then the work should be left undisturbed at least overnight.

Rubber-resin glue is a relatively new and important adhesive. This is what is commonly called "pressure-sensitive synthetic rubber and resin glue," such as Weldwood Contact Cement, or Constantine's Veneer Glue. While it has many important structural uses, its value in veneering is that Micarta and similar laminated plastics can be glued to a wood or plywood kitchen-cabinet counter, table top or other furniture without using any pressure other than that supplied by a rolling pin or other roller. The adhesive is applied with a notched spreader or trowel and allowed to remain exposed to the air for from 15 to 25 minutes before the plastic laminate is laid in place. The greatest precautions must be taken to place the plastic material accurately in position, because the glue holds it so firmly that it is impossible to do any shifting. The plastic laminate is then rolled down in close contact with the supporting surface. Weldwood Contact Cement is specially designed for this purpose.

HINTS ON USING UREA RESIN GLUE

Since urea resin glue is the adhesive most frequently used for veneering, it will be of interest to tell how it is made and give in greater detail the technique of mixing it. When used "straight" — that is, according to the manufacturer's directions — it is very strong and highly moisture resistant. In veneering, however, it often is not necessary to have the glue so strong or moisture resistant, in which case it can be "extended" by adding flour. This reduces the cost of the glue to some extent. The saving is worth while if a lot of veneering is to be done, so the method of mixing the extended glue also will be described.

REQUIRED CONDITIONS FOR USING CASCAMITE OR EXTENDED

40

CASCAMITE. — Although Cascamite joints are stainfree, strong and moisture-resistant, the following conditions are necessary for best results and should be carefully noted:

1. Do not use Cascamite for gluing oily woods (teak, pitch pine, osage orange, yew, lemonwood, etc.), alkaline materials (asbestos, plaster, etc.) or for gluing wood to metal.

2. The material to be glued, and the workroom, should be 70° or warmer.

3. Veneers for veneer pictures, inlays, etc., must be of uniform thickness.

4. Directions for mixing, applying and pressing Cascamite should be followed carefully.

5. Adequate means of applying high pressure should be available.

How To Mix Cascamite Resin Glue (*without flour*).— Use 2 measures (loosely filled) of Cascamite powder to ¾ measure of cold water (60° - 70° F.). Proportions *by weight* are: 10 parts Cascamite powder to 6 parts water. Mix as follows: 1—Pour ½ of the measure of water into any convenient mixing glass, jar or cup. 2—Add the Cascamite powder and stir mixture rapidly until water is absorbed and mix is smooth. Cascamite dissolves immediately and does not thicken and then thin out like Casco Glue. 3—Add balance of water, stir until smooth. The glue is now ready for use.

Spread: 1 lb. of dry Cascamite makes approximately 1-1/3 pints of liquid glue, covers 35 to 45 square feet. For best results, only ½ as thick a film is spread as is used with casein glue, and the glue is applied to one surface only.

How To Mix Extended Cascamite (*with flour*). Make a regular waterproof mix as directed above. Then, for every pound of Cascamite in the waterproof mix, add ½ lb. of flour and up to ½ lb. of extra water. Stir until smooth. The glue is then ready for use.

Important: Use a fresh, white, wheat or rye flour only. Do not use special self-rising flours or flours to which chemicals have been added.

This Extended Cascamite is stainfree, and its dry strength is but little less than that of the waterproof mix. Water-resistance is reduced 1/3 to 1/2 but remains as high as that of average casein glues. Extended Cascamite costs no more to use than casein glue.

Spread: 1 lb. of dry Cascamite, mixed with $\frac{1}{2}$ lb. of flour and $1\frac{1}{4}$ lbs. of water, makes approximately $2\frac{1}{4}$ pints of liquid glue, covers 62 to 77 square feet when spread thin as recommended. Only $\frac{1}{2}$ as heavy a film is spread as is used with Casco No. 2 White Glue, and the glue is applied to one surface only. Liquid Life of Mix: 10 to 12 hours at 70° F. Pressure Time: Hardwoods—12 to 14 hours at 70° F., Softwoods—8 to 10 hours at 70° F.

CAUTION: When mixing Cascamite or Extended Cascamite, avoid copper or brass vessels, or vessels which contain traces of alkali, such as soda or residues of alkaline casein glues.

Use cold water only (at average tap temperatures—60° - 70° F.).

Room temperatures over 70° reduce liquid life of mix. In hot weather, mix only enough for immediate use.

CONTACT-TYPE VENEER GLUE

Although the foregoing adhesives recommended for wood veneers differ in many respects and are individually adapted to special uses and exact usage, they have one thing in common — they require some form of sustained pressure while drying.

An adhesive that does not require clamps or presses of any kind has recently been introduced as Constantine's Veneer Glue. This feature greatly expands the possibilities for the use of veneer. For example, a scratched and stained table top can now be resurfaced with colorful veneers in just a matter of an hour or so without taking anything apart. Chests, cabinets and so on can also be covered quickly with an entirely new surface. This was practically an impossibility when clamps and presses were needed to hold the veneer in place for 12 to 24 hours. With this glue, veneers may be bonded as easily to metal as to wood.

Constantine's Veneer Glue is a liquid, supplied ready to use in pints, quarts, gallons and, for commercial use, in larger sizes to order.

When using this product be certain the temperature of the room and the work are no lower than 70 degrees. Stir contents of can before use. Apply to both surfaces. Allow to dry at least 30 minutes. Extraporous woods require a second coat. Align work perfectly before contact. Press veneer down firmly with rubber roller or rolling pin. No clamps are required.

Complete instructions for using this new glue, and further guidance in the new veneering techniques made possible by this development, have been added to this revised edition as Chapter XVII Veneering Without Clamps, at the end of this book.

PREPARATION OF
CORE AND CROSSBANDS

IN order to understand thoroughly the construction of veneered work, it is necessary to know a few simple, but important, facts about the structure of wood.

FIG. 22—Diagrammatic representation of a wood cell

STRUCTURE OF WOOD —A tree consists of millions of microscopic cells. Some of these are thin-walled and others are thick-walled. Some grow in a vertical direction and others horizontally. In looking at the end of a log, the thick-walled cells appear as circular rings and the thin-walled cells as the lighter wood in between the darker rings. These rings are called the annual rings and, as one is grown each year, the age of the tree can be told by counting the rings. When the tree is cut up into boards or veneers the rings show as straight or wavy lines, called grain.

When the tree is growing, the cells are partly filled with sap, which is a watery liquid. After it is cut into boards or veneer, the sap is evaporated. Some of it is contained in the cells themselves (free water) and some of it in the cell walls, which are porous (imbibed water) (Fig. 22). When the water evaporates from the cell walls they shrink, and the thick-walled cells of course shrink more than the thin-walled. This shrinkage causes the wood to contract and diminish in size. When the cell walls shrink unevenly or too fast, the lumber warps, twists or splits.

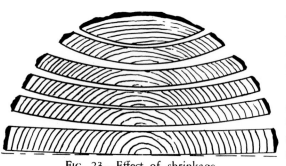

FIG. 23—Effect of shrinkage

The greatest amount of shrinkage takes place along the annual rings. Wood also shrinks across the grain, but little

44

or nothing along the grain. In looking at the boards cut from the log in Fig. 23, it will be seen that the annual rings are longer on the outside part of the boards. They therefore exert a greater pull on that side, causing them to warp or bend away from the heart or center of the log.

If one of these wide boards is cut into smaller widths, it will be seen that the powerful pull of the annual rings is largely broken and the tendency of the narrower boards to warp greatly minimized. This is the principle used in the construction of the cores for plywood or other veneered work.

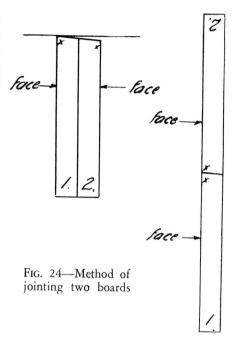

Fig. 24—Method of jointing two boards

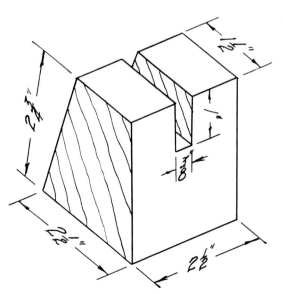

Fig. 25—Block in which to place bar clamps

45

Construction of the Core. — 1. Saw the boards used for cores into widths from 2" to 4" and reverse every other board so that half the boards have the heart side up and half of them the heart side down. In this way the tendency to warp is further minimized (Fig. 3).

2. Number the boards in the way they are going to be glued together and joint their edges.

3. If this is to be done by hand, it is recommended to plane the edges of two adjoining boards at the same time. Clamp them in a bench vise with the numbered

Fig. 26—Gluing boards edge to edge. Thick piece of wood clamped across each end to insure straightness

sides out; then plane them and try the joint by placing one board on top of the other (Fig. 24). The ends should fit tightly, but it is all right if there is a fine opening in the center, because the clamps will draw the boards together and that will make the ends tighter. If the ends do not fit tightly together, the joints will open up after gluing, because the cells are all open in the endwood and consequently dry faster, causing the wood to shrink. That is why boards often have many cracks extending a few inches from their ends.

4. When gluing the boards, place two bar clamps below, one at each end and one on top in the center. If the clamps rest in blocks such as shown in Fig. 25 they are easier to handle.

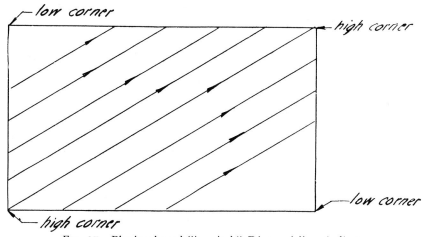

low corner

high corner

low corner

high corner

Fig. 27—Planing board "in wind." Diagonal lines indicate
direction of planing

5. Before gluing, test the joints by tightening the center clamp only. If the boards come together and cannot be moved at the ends by pressing on them with the fingers, the joints are all right.

6. Spread glue on the edges of the boards, place them in position and tighten the center clamp on top first. Then tighten the two other clamps. Bring the surfaces of the boards in alignment by striking those that are too high with a mallet.

7. Test the surface for flatness with a steel square. If necessary, clamp a thick piece of wood having a straight edge across each end of the glued-up core (Fig. 26), but put a piece of paper between the core and the thick piece of wood to prevent the glue from adhering to the latter. Use either hand-screws or C-clamps. If using hand-screws, be careful also to place a piece of paper on the underside of the core.

8. Allow the glue to dry overnight, take the core out of the clamps and remove most of the glue squeezed out of the joints with a chisel.

9. It is recommended to plane the core *across the grain* with a sharp jack plane. Start at one end and plane stroke for stroke until the other end is reached and then return to the starting point. Use a steel square constantly to test the surface for flatness as the planing

47

progresses. Place the square across the grain, along the grain and diagonally from corner to corner.

10. If the square touches on two corners, but not on the opposite two, the board is said to be "in wind." The best way to correct this is to plane diagonally in the direction of one high corner to the other (Fig. 27).

11. When the surface is perfectly flat in all directions, the unevenness of the cross-planing is smoothed off with a very sharp plane set to cut a thin shaving. If the wood is hard or cross-grained, it is preferable to use a cabinet scraper instead of a plane.

12. Gauge the thickness on both edges and ends from the planed surface and plane the other surface in the same manner. It is very important that both surfaces are planed perfectly flat and to the same thickness throughout.

MATERIALS FOR CORES.—If the edges are to be veneered, almost any wood will do for the core provided it does not warp excessively.

Because of its oily nature, pine is not recommended as a core when the gluing is to be done with Cascamite. When pine is used, Casco glue is recommended because it is alkaline and saponifies the surface film of oily woods permitting the glue to "take hold" of the wood fibres. Cascamite will bond to pine, but not as firmly as casein glue.

Serviceable lumber may often be obtained from packing boxes. Large nail holes, knot holes or other defects can be filled with various materials, such as wooden plugs, glue and sawdust, plastic wood, etc. It follows that such repairs must be made level with the surrounding surface.

Pieces of non-warped plywood may also be glued together to give the required core thickness. Artificial woods, for instance, the various compressed fibreboards, or hard or soft fibre sheets, form an excellent core material when Casco Glue is used, because it adheres equally well to hard, smooth surfaces. By using such materials, the exacting work of planing the core is eliminated.

If the edges of the veneered stock are to be shaped, however, the core must be made of the same or similar wood as the face veneers.

CROSSBANDING.—We are now ready to lay the crossbands. These are not always used on the cheaper veneered work, because of the additional labor cost. Crossbanded work, however, is so much superior and the cost of material so low, that this construction is recommended in practically all cases.

1. The crossbands are glued at right angles to the cores, one sheet to each side. If possible, they should be laid without jointing, because a joint is liable to show through a thin face veneer. However, if a joint is unavoidable, it should be made and taped in the same manner as a joint on face veneers. (See Chapter VII, p. 51.) When jointed crossbanding is used, the taped side should be up.

2. Cut the crossbands a little larger than the actual size needed and spread the glue on one of the surfaces of the core, but not on the veneer.

3. Place the veneer on the glued surface and fasten it in position with four veneer pins, one in each corner. Veneer pins are very thin brads with little or no head. Ordinary brads may also be used, for example ¾″ No. 20 or finer. Drive the brads in about ¼″ and then cut them off with a pair of side cutting pliers so that they project about ¼″ above the surface of the veneer. Place a double layer of newspaper over the veneered surface and then a piece of plywood termed the "caul" board. Press the latter down with the hands so that the projecting brads enter into it. Turn the panel and plywood upside down and repeat the process on the other side. Put it in the press or clamp it between boards so that it is well centered, and then tighten the press-screw or clamps all you can. See Chapter VIII for further information about clamping methods.

These operations should be done as quickly as possible. The thin veneer will expand rapidly if allowed time to absorb moisture from the glue. If glued in this expanded condition, shrinkage in drying will cause splits or cracks in the surface.

49

It is very important to treat both surfaces of wood in the same manner. Therefore, if crossbanding is used, both surfaces must be crossbanded and afterwards veneered. If only face veneers are used, both surfaces must be veneered. If one surface is veneered and the other not, the tendency of the veneer is to pull so as to make the veneered surface concave. This is often seen on antique furniture, which was made before the scientific principles involved in veneering were thoroughly understood.

READY-MADE CORE STOCK. While the method of preparing core stock has been described in considerable detail and it is desirable for every woodworker to know something about the process, there is little need for you to make your own core stock unless you wish. Core stock may be purchased ready for veneering, and certain heavy plywood panels may be used. In fact, ordinary fir plywood panels available at any lumber yard will serve the purpose, although there is this difficulty with them: the coarse grain of the rotary-cut fir veneer on the panel may in time show right through a face veneer that is laid over it. For best results it is desirable to lay poplar crossbanding on the fir plywood panel and then follow with the face veneer. Hardboard panels sometimes serve as a core for veneering, especially in the case of inlay pictures. For thin panels, crossbanding alone may be used. For example, a panel may be made with three thicknesses of 1/20" or 1/8" crossbanding and two pieces of 1/28" face veneer; or one center core of 1/8" crossbanding, two pieces of ,1/20" crossbanding and two pieces of face veneer. All sorts of combinations are possible since crossbanding is sold in 1/28", 1/20", 1/8", 3/16" and 1/4" thicknesses.

An inexpensive but excellent ready-made core stock, which is growing in popularity, is Novoply Core Stock. This is manufactured wood panel material made of resin-impregnated wood chips between two 1/16" layers of wood veneer flakes, all fused together with urea resin glue. No crossbanding is required on this type of core.

PREPARING FACE VENEERS FOR GLUING

THE quality and beauty of the finished product is primarily dependent upon the skill and artistic feeling with which the face veneers are selected and combined. Typical veneer combinations are side to side, end to end, four-piece matching, diamond designs, herringbone patterns, borders, centers of various shapes and segmental matching.

FIG. 28—Cutting with a veneer saw

CUTTING AND JOINTING VENEERS. — The tools and equipment needed for this work are very few and inexpensive. A large, old drawing board or discarded table top is suitable for a cutting board, the requirements being that its surface is flat, smooth and fairly soft. The tools needed for the actual cutting of the veneers are a veneer saw (see Fig. 28) and a steel straight-edge or a carpenter's steel square.

Side to Side or Two-Piece Matching consists of two pieces of veneer with identical grain figure (cut from the same flitch) laid so that the two edges from the same side of the log form the joint (Fig. 30).

1. Lay these two pieces on top of each other so that the figure coincides, place the steel square or straight-edge along the line of the cut and draw the saw toward you, holding it perpendicular and against the straight-edge (Fig. 28). As the saw or knife always has a tendency to follow the grain, the veneer when possible, should be placed in such a way that the grain runs slightly toward the straight-edge.

FIG. 30—Side to side matching

2. When the saw has cut through the layers of veneer, their edges should be planed to form a perfect joint. This may be done by clamping them between two boards with straight edges. The edges of the veneer should project a trifle beyond the edges of the boards (Fig. 31).

FIG. 31—Jointing veneers

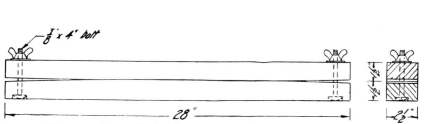

FIG. 32—Clamp for holding veneers while jointing their edges

3. The boards may also be clamped together with a bolt at each end. In this case they should be made of a little heavier stock and their faces rounded slightly so that when the wing nuts are tightened, the veneer will be held as firmly in the center as at the ends (Fig. 32).

4. Veneer held in such a clamp may also be jointed by running it over a power jointer, provided the knives are sharp and a fine cut is taken.

5. Small pieces of veneer may also be jointed by simply clamping them between two boards in a bench vice.

TAPING VENEERS.—1. The two pieces of veneer are now laid on the cutting board with the jointed edges together. To insure a tight joint, veneer pins are driven into both pieces

FIG. 33—Taping a joint

about one inch away from the joint. Slanting the veneer pins toward the joint will tend to bring the two edges closer together.

2. Veneer tape is made of paper or cloth, either perforated or solid. It is usually pregummed. It is sold in rolls about one inch wide and 250 ft. in length. The kind that is used for pasting parcels to-gether instead of tying them with string is satisfactory.

3. Tear off a piece of the tape equal to the length of the joint, moisten the gummed side with a sponge or soft rag and apply the

53

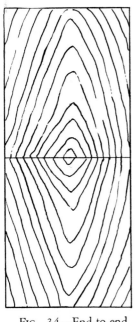

FIG. 34—End-to-end
matching

FIG. 35—Four-piece
matching

tape along the joint. Press it in place with a flat stick rounded at the point (Fig. 33). Place a weight over the joint such as an iron bar, or nail a thin strip of wood over it until the tape is dry and holds the joint firmly together.

End-to-End Matching is another form of two-piece matching. The ends of two pieces of veneer cut from the same flitch are laid together (Fig. 34). This pattern is often

used on drawers. The cutting and taping is done in exactly the same way as side-to-side matching.

Four-Piece Matching is made from four pieces of veneer cut from the same flitch. Each pair is first laid side to side, after which the ends are joined (Fig. 35). This type of matching is usually done with highly figured veneers such as burl walnut or crotch mahogany.

The Angle Mirror is a very great help in predetermining the patterns that can be formed when veneer is cut at different angles. It is useful in developing diamond patterns.

FIG. 36—Angle mirror opened to 90°, showing how four pieces of veneer match

An angle mirror can be made from two pieces of mirror 5″ wide and 12″ long. These are mounted on ¾″ stock of the same width, but about ⅛″ longer than the mirror. The mirrors may be held in place with small pieces of tin nailed to the edges of the wood and bent over the mirror. The ¾″ pieces are hinged together. When the mir-

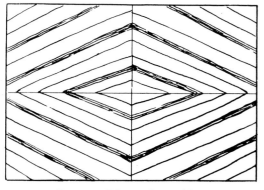

FIG. 37—Diamond matching

ror is opened to 90° a combination of four pieces of veneer is shown in the mirror (Fig. 36). Keeping the mirror at the same opening, but moving it around on the veneer, will show many different combinations possible. Opening the mirror at different angles will show combinations of different numbers of pieces of veneer.

Diamond Matching also consists of matching four pieces of veneer but in this case the four pieces are cut diagonally from the same piece of veneer (Fig. 37). A veneer with striped grain is most suitable for this pattern.

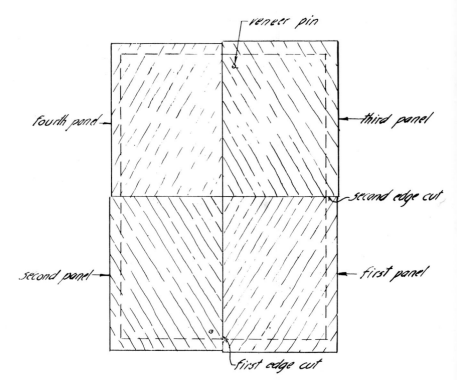

FIG. 38—Method of cutting diamond pattern
(four rectangular pieces)

1. Lay out the design accurately on the piece to be veneered.

2. Then with the aid of the angle mirror, determine the angle at which the veneer is to be cut to produce the best pattern.

3. Cut the veneer at this angle and place the cut edge along the center line marked on the board (Fig. 38).

4. Fasten the veneer in place with a couple of veneer pins and cut it along the other center line.

5. Reverse the sheet of veneer and place the cut edge against the edge first cut. Tack in place and cut along the other center line.

6. Continue in this way until all four pieces have been cut.

7. Joint the long edges as explained on page 51 (Cutting and Jointing Veneers).

8. Tape them together in pairs, then joint the ends and tape these together.

FIG. 39—Diamond matching, X pattern

9. The outside edges are now trimmed to approximate size, a little being allowed for overlapping the sides of the board.

10. When gluing this veneer panel, it must be placed so that its center lines coincide exactly with those marked on the board. This can be accomplished by squaring the center lines on the board over its ends and edges, placing the veneer panel according to these lines and fastening it with only two veneer pins, one at each end and at opposite sides of the long center line. Marking a small circle around the holes left by the pins, both on the veneer and on the board, will help to locate them quickly and exactly when the panel is to be glued (Fig. 38).

There are several variations of the diamond pattern, the most common being the X pattern, which is simply a reversal of the stripe (Fig. 39).

FIG. 40—Diamond matching, triangular

In another form of the diamond design, the four pieces are cut in the form of triangles instead of rectangles (Fig. 40).

57

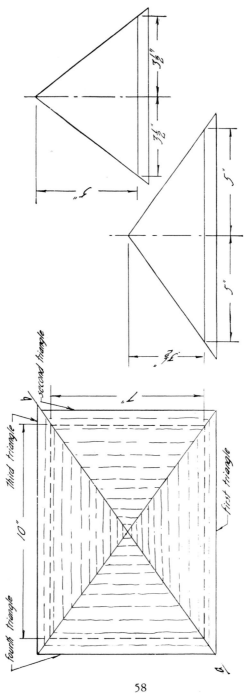

FIG. 41—Method of cutting diamond pattern (four triangular pieces)

In Fig. 41 is shown a rectangular panel where the design is formed by four triangular pieces of veneer. If the panel were square, the triangles would all be of the same size and the grain combination could be determined with the angle mirror. In this case the triangles are of different size and are laid out as follows:

FIG. 42—Diamond matching, herringbone pattern

1. Draw a line on the veneer at right angles to the direction of the grain and mark the triangles as shown, allowing about ½″ for overlapping the edges.

2. Joint and tape the edges of triangles 1 and 2 and of triangles 3 and 4.

3. Now place the two pairs of triangles together and joint them along the diagonal a—b.

4. Fasten them to the panel with veneer pins and tape this last joint.

Herringbone patterns are also variations of the diamond design (Fig. 42).

Centers of Contrasting Wood are often added to diamond patterns. These centers may be diamond shaped, rectangular, square, round or oval. The diamond-shaped center is made as follows:

1. When the four pieces of veneer for a diamond pattern have been cut with the saw, place one on top of the other, but all with the grain running in the same direction.

2. Cut a triangular piece off the corners that meet in the center.

3. Tape a strip of the wood which is to form the center to each piece and trim them again with the saw to the rectangular shape (Fig. 43).

4. Joint them as explained above and tape them together, taking care that the four pieces forming the center meet exactly.

When the design calls for a solid center, square, rectangular, oval or round, the procedure is to make the center first and then fit the other pieces to it.

Borders are simply frames placed around any design. They are very often used around diamond patterns. Borders may be made either with the grain running side to side (Fig. 44), which is the long way of the wood, or end to end (Fig. 45), which is the short way of the wood. Borders add greatly to the beauty of the design, especially when they run at right angles to the side grain or the short way of the wood.

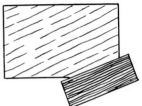

FIG. 43—Forming a diamond center

1. In this case a number of strips are cut from a striped piece of veneer at right angles to the stripe.

2. These are then jointed and taped together side to side, forming one continuous band. On account of the brittleness of the short grain, it is advisable to glue a piece of tape across the entire band.

3. The end grain of the border is jointed together with the side grain of the veneer to which it is to be taped.

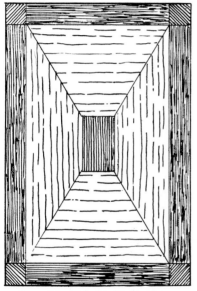

FIG. 44—Side-to-side border, rectangular center

4. Lay the design out in pencil on the panel which is to be veneered. Trim the center veneer to exact size and tack it in place with a couple of veneer pins. Tape the border in place, one side at a time, and cut the miter joints in the corners according to the pencil lines marked. The border should be cut so that it overlaps the edges of the panel.

5. Lines of inlay are often used in combination with borders. They are simply laid up to the jointed edges and taped in place.

Segmental Matching is an elaboration of the diamond patterns and consists of more than four pieces of veneer usually triangular in shape and meeting in a central point such as is shown in the photo of the octagon top (Fig. 60). Further subdivision of this pattern is called a sunburst.

Segmental veneers are a little more difficult to match than the types described so far. The veneers for the octagonal top were cut as follows:

1. The figured maple was first cut to width, after which the border made from East Indian rosewood was cut as described above, jointed

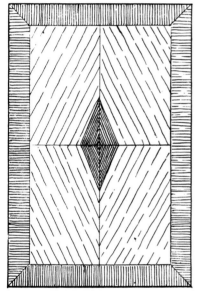

and taped to both sides of the maple veneer (Fig. 46).

2. The pattern was then drawn on the board to be veneered and the triangle laid out on one end of the veneer. It is very important that both legs of the triangle are exactly the same length, as the border and center otherwise will not fit.

3. Cut the first triangle and fasten it in place temporarily with a couple of veneer pins.

4. Then lay the veneer up to the edge of this triangle and mark and cut the second triangle. Be careful to see that the border and center fit perfectly.

FIG. 45—End-to-end border, diamond center

5. Remove the veneer pins from the first triangle and joint the two adjoining edges. Fasten the two triangles temporarily to the board, mark and cut the next two and continue until all eight are cut.

6. Tape four triangles together on each side of one of the center lines. Then joint the two halves and tape the last joint.

Be careful not to get too many layers of tape crossing each other.

All taping must be done on one side.

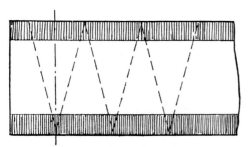

FIG. 46—Forming an octagonal top pattern with border

Plain Figured Veneers are cut for the reverse side. These are prepared and laid in the same manner as the crossbands, but at right angles to the crossbands.

All veneers have what is termed a "right" or "tight" and a "wrong" or "loose" side. When a single piece of veneer is laid, glue should be applied to the loose side. When veneer is matched, this of course is impossible, because half the pieces are reversed. The loose side of a piece of veneer may be found by rubbing a finger over its end (Fig. 47). On one side small chips will break off. This is the loose side.

REPAIRING AND STRAIGHTENING CURLED VENEERS.

—Veneers are often cracked, especially at the ends. Such cracks can be repaired by gluing a piece of veneer tape over them, and this should be done before they are cut and laid.

Crotch and burl veneers are usually very brittle and curly. They may be straightened by wetting them with hot water and placing them be-

FIG. 47—Rubbing finger over end of veneer to determine right or wrong side

tween two boards, which are then clamped together or weighted.

If the boards are heated, either in the sun or against a radiator, it will help to shrink the veneers back to their original size.

On account of the brittleness of such veneers, and their tendency to reassume their former curly shape as soon as they are left without clamps, it is advisable to glue them to a piece of strong, heavy paper or, better still, to a piece of straight-grained veneer. In this case the grain of the two veneers must run parallel.

In this way the difficulties of cutting, jointing and laying these veneers are largely overcome.

SIZING OF CROTCH AND BURL VENEERS.—These brittle veneers are made sufficiently flexible and strong for safe handling by sizing with a mixture of (1) adhesive, for strength, (2) glycerine, for flexibility, and (3) alcohol, for quick drying. The following formula is recommended:

Cascamite Resin Powder	2 measures	(1 part by weight)
Flour	1 measure	(½ part by weight)
Water	3 measures	(2¾ parts by weight)
Glycerine	1½ measures	(1¼ parts by weight)
Alcohol	½ to 1 measure	(1/3 - 2/3 parts by weight)

This solution should be used cold.

Use a suitable trough so that the veneers can be completely immersed for a minute or two. The veneers should then be stood on end to drain, and as soon as the surface is dry to the touch, they should be placed between dry softwood caul boards (preferably basswood or poplar), which have been warmed. These boards should be weighted to keep the veneers flat. After 24 hours the veneers should be transferred to another set of dry softwood boards. In this way the veneers are dried and shrunk slowly. At the end of the treatment they should be flat, strong and flexible, thus making the cutting, jointing and laying of these normally brittle veneers an easy matter.

GLUING VENEERS UNDER PRESSURE

VENEERS must be glued under a strong pressure uniformly distributed over the entire surface. For good results with any glue, and especially in gluing with Cascamite, there must be perfect contact of wood to wood between the surfaces to be glued. The best means of applying such pressure is with a veneer press.

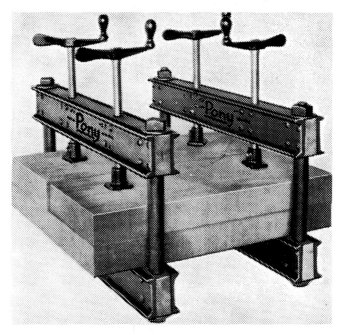

FIG. 48—"Pony" veneer press

Veneer presses used in commercial plants are generally huge, expensive pieces of machinery built up of steel I-beams and plates and tightened by means of hand or power-driven screws or by hydraulic plungers.

For small commercial shops, school shops or home woodworkers, smaller size presses, embodying the same structural features as the larger ones are now on the market. Such a press is shown in Fig. 48.

The press consists of two "Pony" veneer press frames, each being an independent unit. The frames are available in two sizes. One has an inside capacity of 18" clear width, 6" clear height. The other will clamp work that is fully 36" wide and is equipped with four 11/16" diameter press screws.

A veneer press can be constructed of wood without difficulty and at considerable saving since "Pony" press screws can be obtained by themselves. Typical construction of such a press is shown in Fig. 49.

The size of the frames depends, naturally, upon the work to be done. The strain, especially on top member A, as shown in drawing No. 1, is considerable. It is a good rule to make frame members *oversize* rather than undersize. Oak, maple, birch or other very hard wood should be used if possible, but hard yellow pine, or other sound, strong, straight-grained lumber will serve if that is all that is available. For frames to take a panel 36" wide (with some allowance for trimming), stock 4 x 4's, which are about 3⅝" x 3⅝", are the *lightest* recommended.

Joints may be made as in drawing No. 1. If, however, a side-opening press is desired for gluing long work, one side member of each frame can be pivoted as shown in drawing No. 3 so that it may be opened by removing the top bolt. The work then slides in from the side rather than the end of the row of press frames.

The length of the side members is governed by the distance the selected screw will travel through the upper cross member, plus the thickness of the work and the bed and cauls used.

The bed may be a thick plywood panel, a metal plate, or a frame made as shown in drawing No. 4 and covered by laying on it a ¾ thick plywood panel, a sheet of thick, tempered hardboard, or a metal plate.

For gluing wide panels, one press frame is normally used for each 9" of length, but the frames, if not fastened permanently to the bed, may be shifted closer or farther apart, depending upon circumstances and the pressure required. For average work, find the number of square inches in the panel and divide by 80. This will give the number of

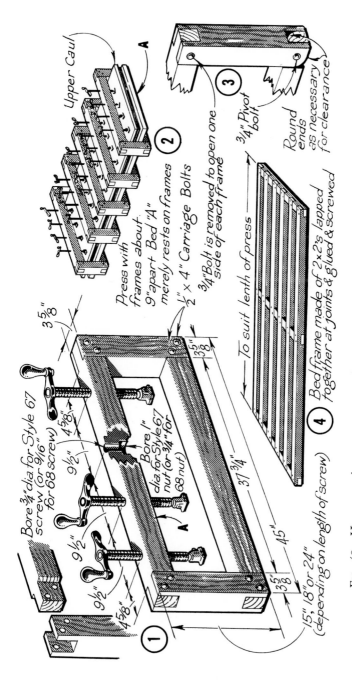

Upper Caul

③ 3/4" Pivot bolt

Round ends as necessary for clearance

② Press with frames about 9" apart Bed "A" merely rests on frames

1/2" x 4" Carriage Bolts

3/4" Bolt is removed to open one side of each frame

A

To suit length of press

④ Bed frame made of 2x2's lapped together at joints & glued & screwed

Bore 3/4" dia. for Style 67 screw (or 9/16" for 68 screw)

4 5/8"

9 1/2"

9 1/2"

9 1/2"

9 1/2"

4 5/8"

3 5/8"

Bore 1" dia. for Style 67 nut (or 3/4" for 68 nut)

A

15", 18" or 24" (depending on length of screw)

37 3/4"

45"

35 3/8"

3 5/8"

35 3/8"

3 5/8"

①

Fig. 49—How to make a veneer press frame with "Pony" press screws; arrangement of frames to form a press; a strong, durable type of bed frame; and detail of a side-opening frame

press screws (not frames) required — that is, one press screw for each 80 square inches.

A smaller press is readily made of stock 2 x 3's. Each frame requires two pieces 22¼" long and two pieces 12½" long. The longer members, which form the top and bottom of the frame, are placed edge up and are set into open mortises cut in the ends of the shorter side members. Two ½" diameter "Pony" press screws are required for each frame. This press will take work up to 18" wide, just like the one shown in Fig. No. 48.

Much small work such as panels, boxes, etc. can even be successfully veneered without a press. In such cases the veneered work is placed between caul boards ⅞" or more in thickness and only ordinary handscrews or C-clamps are used, Fig. 50. To insure an absolutely flat surface, one of the caul boards may be replaced with a piece of ¼" plywood placed on a machined surface such as a bandsaw table. The veneered work is then clamped to that as shown in Fig. 51.

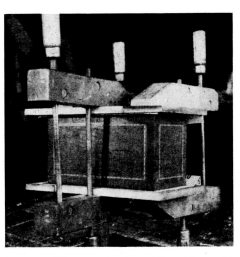

Cauls are made of wood, fibre or metal. They are placed between the veneered stock and the plates of the press, as well as between different layers of veneered stock. Plywood or compressed fibre panels cut to the size of the press are very satisfactory. Metal cauls are easily dented, and in this condition injure the surface of face veneers.

FIG. 50—Veneers glued to sides of box with ordinary handscrews used as clamps

It is important that the cauls be kept clean, as any foreign matter like hardened glue will make dents in the veneered surface. Cauls are

FIG. 51—Veneering small tray by
clamping it to band saw table

sometimes oiled or soaped to prevent glue from adhering to them. Wood caul boards should have a smooth, close-textured surface. Birch or maple panels are recommended.

PLACING VENEERED STOCK IN THE PRESS.—Having prepared the face and plain veneers, these may be glued at the same time. The following order of procedure is recommended:

1. Scrape off any veneer tape that may have been used on the crossbands. Spread a sufficient quantity of glue on the surface to which the plain veneer is to be glued. Be sure there is enough glue at the edges.

2. Lay the veneer on the glued surface, remembering that the taped side of the veneer should always be out. If the taped side is glued, the paper is liable to split, thereby loosening the veneer. Press the veneer down by hand and fasten it with four veneer pins (Fig. 52). Cut the pins off near the surface.

3. Reverse the board, spread glue on the face side, apply the face veneer, and nail it in place, being careful to see that it is correctly placed (see page 57).

4. Place a double sheet of newspaper over each veneered surface, place the board between two cauls and put it in the press. See that it is well centered and apply the pressure.

FIG. 52—Gluing and tacking veneer

5. This work should be done as quickly as possible. When Casca-mite is used, too long an assembly period may result in the thin glue film drying out. With certain other glues, the veneers may swell by absorbing moisture from the glue.

6. When using any glue that may stain, do not let panel remain in the press over 6 hours as this may aggravate the staining. When using Cascamite, allow full time and apply all pressure possible. No risk of glue stain is encountered with Cascamite, and veneers may remain under pressure overnight.

7. When the panel is removed from the press, it is best to clamp one or two pieces of wood across it for a day or two to prevent the possibility of warping until the glue moisture dries out thoroughly.

8. Several boards of the same size may be veneered at the same time if they are centered exactly over each other. When they are taken from the press, small sticks about 3/4" square should be placed in line between them, one above the other, to allow the air to circulate around

them while drying. They may all be clamped together with four hand-screws.

9. Boards of different sizes should never be veneered at the same time.

GLUE STAIN

Ordinary casein glues are usually highly water resisting, and also very alkaline. Certain woods, especially mahogany, oak, redwood and others, contain a high percentage of tannic acid. Discoloration, therefore, frequently occurs along edge joints from the reaction of the alkaline glue with the acid wood.

Very thin, highly figured face veneers contain a large amount of end grain and are therefore subject to a greater penetration of glue moisture with the consequent danger of discoloration. When gluing such veneers, the following precautions should be observed:

1. Mix a heavier bodied glue than usual, taking one quarter of a pound less of water to each pound of dry glue powder in the case of urea resin or casein glues.

2. Spread a thin, even film of glue. To do this, use a stiff brush.

3. Place old newspapers over face veneer as directed on page 68 before placing panel in press. This acts as blotting paper for the glue moisture.

4. Remove panel from pressure after only two hours.

HOW TO REMOVE GLUE STAIN.—If glue stain does occur, it can be removed by sponging the stained surface of the panel with a solution of oxalic acid. Secure oxalic acid crystals from a drug store. Dissolve one part in ten parts of hot water. Use when cool. This bleaching solution will keep indefinitely. Because it is clear, like water, and is a poison, the bottle must be labeled "*poison.*"

VENEERING CURVED WORK

URVED work, such as a door for a small cabinet, can not only be veneered in the press described in the preceding chapter, but can actually be bent to the desired shape in this press.

The manner in which this is done will be easily understood from the accompanying drawing (Fig. 53), in which the door is shown glued and bent to shape between a number of small square sticks supported in two cradles, one convex and the other concave.

1. The first thing to do is to determine the thickness of the door and the amount of curvature, and then make a full size drawing of its cross-section, the small squared sticks, called "tambours," and the cradles. It will readily be seen that the curvature of the cradles is dependent both on the curvature of the door and its thickness.

2. The pieces forming the cradles can be made from 7/8" wood. If three are needed, nail these together and saw the curve. They should be spaced from 8" to 10" apart and may be held together with dowels.

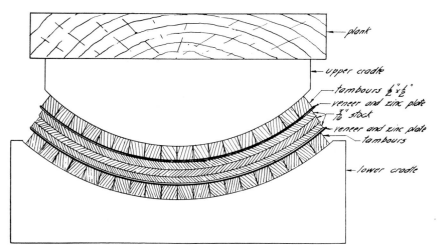

FIG. 53—Curved door assembly showing clamping device

Fig. 54—Curved door, tambours, cradles and zinc plates after
removal from press

3. The tambours are made about ½″ square and a little longer than the door to be glued. They are held loosely together with cord passed through holes bored in them. In this way, they adjust themselves to any curvature.

4. The core is made of three or four layers of ⅛″ single ply poplar veneer. These are placed one on top of the other with the grain running in the same direction. The inside and outside surfaces are covered with 1/20″ crossbanding, which as in ordinary veneering, is placed at right angles to the core.

5. Place one sheet of crossbanding in position and spread the glue quickly on both sides of each core veneer. Place the second sheet of crossbanding on top of the pile and drive a nail at each end through all the layers of veneer.

6. Place a thin metal sheet, or thin, hard fibreboard, on both sides of the glued-up work and put it in the press between the cradles. Be careful to place two or three sheets of newspaper on the veneer. It is very important that the work is accurately centered. To do this, draw center lines on the cradles and on the stock to be bent. Apply pressure gradually. The metal sheet or thin fibreboard below the door will prevent the veneer from cracking as it is being bent into shape.

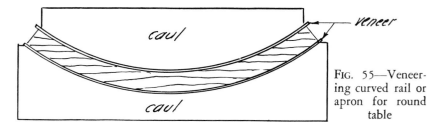

FIG. 55—Veneering curved rail or apron for round table

7. Leave the work overnight in the press. When it is removed (Fig. 54) the edges and ends are trimmed. A piece of ½″ stock is then glued to both edges and smoothed flush with both surfaces, after which the face veneers are glued at right angles to the crossbands, using the clamping method described above. The solid strips of wood are glued to the edges of the door to give it a finished appearance and to make it easier to put on hinges and lock.

8. When solid, curved stock is to be veneered, such as the drawer of a commode or the apron of a small round table (Fig. 55), it should be band-sawed very accurately and the waste pieces retained and used for cauls.

9. When irregularly curved surfaces are to be veneered, bags filled with sand, bran or sawdust are often used to distribute the pressure. The bag should be put in a box made for the purpose (Fig. 56). The surface to be veneered is first pressed against it to form the shape. The veneer is then fastened with pins, and pressure applied.

10. Cauls may also be cast of plaster of Paris. Excelsior mixed into the wet plaster adds considerably to its strength.

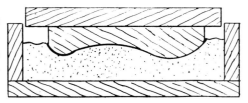

FIG. 56—Veneering curved stock, using sandbag in box

VENEERING WOOD WITH METAL
AND OTHER MATERIALS

USEFUL and decorative panels can be made of materials other than wood. The core, made of wood in the usual way, and with a crossbanding glued to it, may be faced with a variety of materials, such as linoleum or compressed fibreboard, for kitchen or office table tops; metal, of various kinds; laminated resinoids, which is the general descriptive term applying to such materials as Formica, Micarta, Panelyte, etc. Fireproof panels are made by using asbestos slate instead of wood for cores.

FIG. 57—Four Micarta patterns: two wood grains, pearl and linen

The following suggestions apply to the materials mentioned:

LINOLEUM OR COMPRESSED FIBREBOARD. — Glue the same as wood veneer, using Casco Grade "A" Glue, or use Weldwood Contact Cement, Armstrong's D-243 or other contact-adhering cement and merely roll down the material.

Fig. 58—Coffee table by Pascoe with Micarta Truwood top

METAL.—A zinc-protected sheet is desirable, to avoid the problem of corrosion. "Galvaneal" and "Paintgrip" are the trade names of galvanized sheet steels, which glue well, and provide a good surface for paint.

Since dry heat expands metal and shrinks wood, these materials constantly move in opposite directions with temperature changes. Consequently, the adhesive used must have the ability to stretch slightly without losing strength. A synthetic rubber and resin adhesive such as Armstrong's D-243 is excellent for bonding metal to wood and other materials. Casco Flexible Cement, made with casein and latex, was specially developed for this type of work and also has the ability to hold tightly to metal, plastics and other polished surfaces to which ordinary glues do not "take."

Casco Flexible Cement can be used for veneering to metal in either of 2 ways: 1—As it comes from the can. This makes a joint with maximum flexibility. 2—By mixing 1 measure of standard mix of

Casco Grade "A" with 1 measure of cement. This gives less flexibility with greater strength.

Before gluing, remove any trace of oil from the surface of the metal with a cloth soaked in benzine or alcohol. Spread cement with a stiff brush and press in usual way.

Copper, aluminum, etc., can be glued by the above method.

RESINOIDS.—Usually these consist of thin sheets of felt, impregnated with a phenolic resin, made hard and durable by great pressure and heat. A variety of patterns are imprinted into the surface of these materials; for instance, the grain and design of various veneers; flowered or figured designs; imitation marble, etc.

Laminated plastics, as they are commonly called, introduce a special problem because they are so often applied to built-in kitchen-cabinet counters, built-in combination lavatory-vanities, built-in breakfast-nook tables, and the like. The Micarta or other laminate is therefore applied after the article has been assembled in place, and it is difficult to apply adequate clamping pressure if one of the ordinary veneering adhesives is used. It was to overcome this problem that pressure-sensitive or contact cements were developed, one of which is Weldwood Contact Cement.

If it is desired to veneer individual panels with a laminated plastic and a veneer press is available, then a heavy-bodied casein glue may be used, but it is advisable to roughen the underside of the laminated plastic sheet slightly with sandpaper. Maximum pressure should be applied and the panel or panels should be left in the press overnight.

ASBESTOS.—The surface should be sanded smooth. The asbestos should be treated as a wood core and a soft-textured crossbanding veneer glued to it in the usual way. Use Casco Grade "A" Casein Glue. Urea resin glues are not recommended for gluing alkaline material such as asbestos, plaster, gypsum, etc.

VENEERING DEFECTS

THE most common defects that are likely to occur in veneering are blisters, loose edges and warped panels.

A blister on a veneered panel is very similar in appearance to a blister on the hand and indicates that the veneer has become unglued at that point. It may show up when the panel is removed from the press or it may appear later. The causes of a blister are usually too little glue or too long time elapsing between spreading the glue and placing the panel under pressure. A blister may be repaired as follows:

1. Slit the blister near its center with a very sharp and thin knife blade.

2. Press one-half of the blister down, while introducing some quick-setting, heat-sensitive glue such as Elmer's Glue-All or hot animal glue under the other half with a knife blade. Repeat this process on the other half of the blister.

3. Wet the blister with water and press it down with a flatiron heated to the usual temperature for pressing clothes. The water softens the veneer and the warmth of the flatiron remelts the now chilled glue. Cover the blister with wax paper and lay on a weight for a few minutes. Casco or Cascamite may also be used, but apply pressure until the glue sets.

Loose edges may be caused by uneven or insufficient pressure, too quick removal from the press, too little glue or too long time elapsing between pressing and spreading.

Uneven pressure often results from using veneers of unequal thickness. The standard domestic veneer is 1/28″ in thickness, but some imported veneers are only 1/32″ in thickness. If possible, always use veneers of uniform thickness for the same panel, but if veneers of different thicknesses must be used, the pressure may be evenly distributed if a piece of soft-textured fibreboard is placed between the caul and the panel.

Loose edges may be repaired by introducing a little glue under the veneer with a knife blade. Either Elmer's Glue-All, Casco or Cascamite may be used. The edges should be clamped in the press or with hand screws.

Warped panels may be caused by unbalanced construction or unseasoned wood (see preparation of core and crossbands, page 46), improper stacking after removal from press (see drying and stacking after taking from press, page 69), or a too damp or too cold gluing room. Dampness and cold retard the setting of the glue. Warped panels usually cannot be repaired.

Repairing veneered surfaces, and for that matter, repairing a host of furniture defects has been greatly simplified by the

FIG. 58a — Glue injector useful in repairs

introduction of a product called a glue injector. This little tool consists of a barrel which holds glue, and a plunger which forces a controlled amount of glue through a very fine nozzle. So that glue can be injected deep into a loose joint without taking the joint apart, a hole is made with a 1/16" drill point which comes in the handle of the injector. Putting glue exactly where you want it not only assures the success of a repair to a veneered surface or furniture joint, but also avoids the mess of more primitive methods and prevents glue stains on exposed areas of wood.

PREPARING VENEERED WORK
FOR FINISHING

TRIMMING EDGES.—When the veneered panel has dried for a day or two after removal from the press, the overlapping veneer should be trimmed flush with the edges.

This may be done with a sharp knife or chisel or with a saw. It is advisable to trim the edges of the plain back veneer first, because it is then easier to get at the face veneer. If a border of end to side grain has been used, as in the octagonal top (Fig. 60), it is advisable to place the top face down on the cutting board and trim the veneer with a sharp dovetail or fine back saw (Fig. 59).

SHAPING EDGES.—The edges may now be finished either by shaping them or by veneering them. When the edges are to be shaped, it follows that the core and crossbands are made of the same or similar wood that can be stained to match these.

In Fig. 61 are shown three ways of shaping the edges. If a shaper is available, this may of course be done in many other ways, but the ones illustrated can be worked out very easily by hand.

FIG. 59—Trimming overlapping veneer with dovetail saw

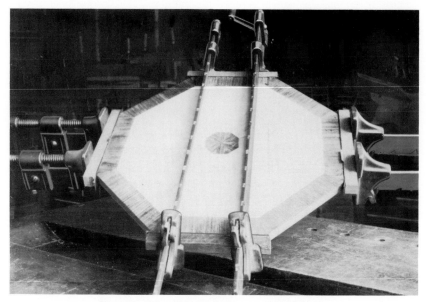

FIG. 60—Veneering edges on octagonal top

1. In A it is recommended first to square the edges and then gauge a pencil line on both surfaces, about 3/16″ from the edge. Using a spokeshave, work out the rough shape and smooth it with a cabinet scraper and sandpaper.

2. In B it is also advisable to work from a square edge. The beads can be made with a scratch stock (see Fig. 62) fitted with a cutter of the desired shape.

3. In C first cut or plane a rabbet, as shown by the dotted lines. This can easily be done on a small circular saw or with a rabbet plane. Then round the edge with a block plane. It is advisable to clamp a piece of thin stock to the top in order to protect the corner and avoid damaging it with the plane.

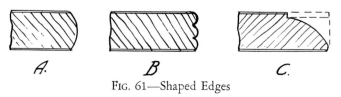

A.   *B*   *C.*

FIG. 61—Shaped Edges

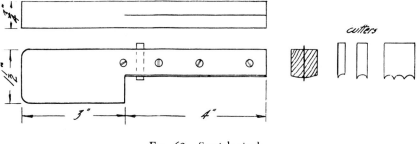

cutters

FIG. 62—Scratch stock

4. It is also recommended to make a template of stiff cardboard, which should be used frequently while planing the edge so that its shape will be uniform. Finish with scraper and sandpaper.

VENEERING EDGES.—1. If the edges are to be veneered, they should first be planed perfectly flat and smooth.

2. The veneer is then prepared in the usual way. The grain may run either parallel to the edges or across them. In the latter case narrow strips are cut across the grain and taped together like borders (see page 60). In either case the veneer should be cut wide enough to overlap the edges.

3. Veneers are glued to the edges as follows: Fasten them in place with veneer pins, protect them with soft wood blocks and clamp them simultaneously to two opposite edges with bar clamps (Fig. 60). It is well to size endwood with a thinner mixture of glue and let it dry before applying the regular glue mixture. The glue closes the open pores in the endwood.

4. When all the edges have been veneered, the part projecting over the surfaces is carefully trimmed off with a plane and sandpaper.

5. The sharp corners between veneered surfaces and edges are often finished by a piece of black or satin line inlay about ⅛" square. After the face veneers have been glued and trimmed flush with the edges a recess is cut for the line with a tool called a scratch stock.

6. A scratch stock is one of those tools that can easily be made by

81

any woodworker. It consists simply of a piece of hardwood about ⅞″ thick, 1½″ wide and 7″ long, shaped as shown in the drawing (Fig. 62). It has a slit from the end to the handle into which a thin steel cutter can be fastened. These cutters are made from broken saw blades filed into the desired shape.

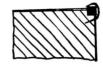

Fig. 63 — Veneer pins holding corner inlay in place while gluing

7. For cutting across the grain, a cutter having a very sharp point is used. After this line is scored, a cutter having a square edge is used for scraping out the recess.

8. If a ⅛″ x ⅛″ line is to be inlaid, the recess should be a little less than ⅛″, both in width and depth, to allow for sanding.

9. The line is now mitered at the corners and glued into the recess. It is held in place by veneer pins driven into the edge and bent over it (Fig. 63) or with veneer tape.

10. When dry, the veneer pins are removed and the line inlay scraped or sanded flush and its edge rounded.

INLAY.—1. While line inlay can often be taped together with the face veneers, intricate patterns, such as that shown on the Jewel Box (page 101), have to be inlaid after the veneer is glued. This is done pretty much in the same way as the edge inlay described above.

2. The scratch stock is used for cutting the recesses. Cutters with two sharp points are used for scoring the wood and a square-edged cutter for removing the wood between the two lines scored. If a Stanley Electric Router is available, it should, of course, be used for this and all similar recessing and molding operations.

3. The inlay lines, which are of the same thickness as the veneer, should fit very tightly in the grooves cut for them. They are mitered in the corners. Apply glue to the line only and then force it into the groove by rubbing the head of a hammer over it. Allow at least 12 hours for drying and then sand smooth. The moisture from the glue causes the lines to swell. If sanded too soon, the subsequent contraction will cause them to shrink below the surface.

FIG. 64—Veneer inlays

Insets are center or corner decorations made up of several pieces of different colored woods sawed out and combined into various designs as flowers, sea shells, geometrical patterns, etc.

Both lines and insets (Fig. 64) are sold by manufacturers of marquetry. Insets are glued to paper and set in the center of a piece of veneer to protect their edges.

1. To inlay the inset, remove the veneer around it by cutting it into small strips with a sharp pocket knife. Clean off any paper from the edges by scraping lightly with the knife or a fine file.

2. If the inset is to be placed in the center of a top or panel, locate its position by drawing center lines both on the panel and the papered side of the inset.

3. Place the inset face down, so that the center lines coincide, and mark its outline with a very sharp, hard pencil.

4. Cut around this outline with a sharp knife or chisels and gouges of the proper curvature. Remove the veneer inside the outline with a router plane. As insets are usually manufactured to the same standard thickness as sliced veneer ($1/28''$), only the layer of face veneer is cut away.

5. Glue the inset face down, that is, with the papered side up. Place a piece of paper over the inset and a block of soft wood on this, and clamp with a handscrew.

When a small electric router is available, recesses for lines and insets may be cut with greater facility.

PREPARING THE SURFACES FOR FINISHING.—After the work has been completed and has had time to dry thoroughly, the surfaces must be cleaned, smoothed and prepared for the finishing coats.

1. The first thing to do is to remove every bit of paper from the joints taped together and from any inset used. This may be done by sanding or by moistening the paper with a little water and scraping it off with a handscraper or putty knife. The water will cause the cells on the surface of the veneer to swell slightly. It is therefore best to use as little water as possible, and to allow some time for drying after the paper has been removed.

2. If there are any dents or nicks in the surface, it is well to wet them with hot water at this time. In most cases the cells will absorb enough water to swell to their original size.

3. The veneer pins should either be removed or cut off and set below the surface. The holes made by them can be filled with stick shellac which resembles sealing wax and is melted by holding a heated knife, spatula or iron against it. It hardens immediately and is leveled off with the surface with a sharp chisel and sandpaper.

4. As a rule, sliced veneers only 1/28″ thick should not be scraped. When inlays are used, however, it may be necessary to go over them with a *very sharp* handscraper. Only a few very fine cuts can be taken.

5. The veneer should now be sanded with No. ½ or No. 0 sandpaper. Fold the sandpaper over a sanding cork or a piece of soft wood when sanding flat surfaces. *Always sand with the grain.* Sanding across the grain leaves some very objectionable scratches that show badly through any finish. Finish sanding with No. 2/0 sandpaper.

6. If spots of grease or oil have inadvertently come on the surface, they may be removed with a piece of clean waste moistened with naptha.

7. Give the surface a final thorough inspection, remembering a perfect finish can only be produced on a perfect surface, and that any little imperfection in the surface will show as if magnified through the finish.

INLAID PICTURES

A N INLAID picture is really a piece of marquetry work, which, as described on page 10, is a sheet of veneer inlaid with other veneers of the same thickness, but of different colors. Combining these so that a picture is formed, is in effect to paint with wood instead of with oil or water colors. Detailed instructions for making inlaid pictures are contained in a 25-cent booklet, *The Secrets of Making Inlay Pictures,* a Constantine publication. This also lists 50 pictures of various sizes for which the veneers, master drawings and borders are available in construction-kit form.

Marquetry pictures are made commercially as follows: The tracing is cut along the lines forming the picture into its component parts. Each part is glued to the upper layer of about 25 veneers nailed together to form one solid block. These blocks are then cut on a special power jig saw around the edges of the paper glued to it. The pieces are then fitted together like a jig saw puzzle and glued to a piece of paper. In this way 25 identical pictures are made, all parts, large or small, fitting perfectly together.

Fig. 65—Veneers nailed together ready for sawing

As this method naturally requires a high degree of skill, the following simpler method is recommended for the beginner.

1. Procure a piece of veneer, which is a little larger than the completed picture, for each color required.

2. Arrange these veneers so that the grain in some runs horizontally, in others vertically, and in still others obliquely according to the requirements of the design, Fig. 65.

3. Place a piece of ⅛″ poplar on top and one on bottom, nail all the pieces together along the edges and paste your tracing on one of the outside poplar veneers.

4. Saw carefully along all the lines of the design, using either a hand or a power jig saw. The finer the saw blade used, the closer the pieces will fit.

5. The various pieces of veneer, previously selected according to color and grain, are now fitted together and glued to a piece of paper.

6. When dry, the edges are squared with a plane and a suitable border of striped veneer resembling a picture frame, Fig. 66, is fitted around the picture (see page 60).

7. The completed picture is glued with the papered side up to a crossbanded core.

FIG. 66—Completed picture with veneer frame
around it

WOOD FINISHING

A GOOD finish is of the utmost importance in bringing out the inherent beauties in veneers. Finishing operations can be classified under four general headings: staining or coloring the wood, filling the pores, applying the transparent coats, rubbing and polishing. These will be briefly discussed, but much more complete information, especially in respect to professional materials and methods, will be found in the *Constantine Wood-Finishing Manual*.

STAINING.—Many woods are endowed by nature with such a beautiful, rich color or markings that they should not be stained at all. Others, like mahogany, only obtain their brownish, red color with age. Maple likewise only takes on its characteristic golden color with age. It is to imitate such richer colors that stain is chiefly used on veneers.

1. Stains are of different kinds: spirit stains, oil stains, water stains and non-grain-raising stains. Of these, the last two are to be preferred because they are clear, penetrate deeply and are easy to apply.

2. The only difficulty with water stains is that they raise the grain. This can be overcome by moistening the veneer with water and re-sanding when dry.

3. Water stains are sold in powder form. This powder is dissolved in hot water in the proportions specified by the manufacturer. By varying these proportions darker or lighter shades may be obtained.

4. Brush only with the grain and along the entire surface to prevent laps. When the brush is full, begin on the unfinished part of the surface and work toward the part already stained.

5. Water stain should be brushed until almost dry, except when high-lighting is desired. In this case the part that is to be lighter, such as the center of a panel, is wiped with a rag or a piece of waste.

6. When inlay or light veneers have been used in combination with mahogany veneer, it is advisable to apply a stain made of powdered lime dissolved in water. The lime and tannic acid contained in all mahogany wood react chemically and give the wood a rich red color, the darkness of the shade depending upon the strength of the solution. The lime does not affect the lighter woods.

7. Before applying the lime water it is better to strain the undissolved lime out of the solution. When dry, the surface looks as if it has been whitewashed. It is cleaned off with a rag, a piece of cotton waste or a stiff brush. The white particles in the pores disappear when the surface is rubbed with a little boiled linseed oil thinned with turpentine.

8. If the color is not dark enough, a second application or a stronger lime solution is necessary. If it becomes too dark, it may be lightened with a solution of oxalic acid—one part of acid to ten parts of water.

FILLING THE PORES.—Porous woods such as oak, or to a less degree mahogany and walnut, should be filled with a paste wood filler in order to produce a smoother surface.

1. Paste wood filler is made of silex ground in oil, shellac and various other gums. It may be obtained in various colors.

2. To prepare wood filler for use, dig a lump out of the can and thin it with turpentine until it has the consistency of cream. Apply it liberally and brush it well into the pores of the wood. When it becomes flat in appearance after 10 or 15 minutes, rub it across the grain with a piece of burlap, tow or any coarse rags, forcing it well into the pores.

3. The surplus may be cleaned off by wiping with the grain or by scraping it off with a putty knife with rounded edges.

4. When wiping with the grain, some of the filler is lifted out of the pores. When using the putty knife, the filler is pressed well into the pores, but a thin film is left on the surface. This may be removed the following day by sanding the surface lightly with No. 2/0 sandpaper and rubbing it with a rag moistened with turpentine.

5. Hardwoods like maple and most tropical woods, are so dense and have such small pores that no filling is necessary. Sometimes woods of this kind are given a coat of thin shellac as a filler. But if the surface is to be varnished, no shellac undercoating is to be given.

VARNISHING.—-Varnish is made in many grades and differs a great deal. Some require 48 hours for drying and some dry dust-free in a few hours. The latter kind are recommended because they can be applied without the need of a dust-proof finishing room.

1. When using a rubbing varnish, the best results are obtained when it is applied directly over the filler or over a thin undercoating of shellac sanded smooth.

2. Wipe the surface clean with a rag moistened with turpentine and apply the varnish as it comes from the can, spreading it over the surface with light, even strokes. The room in which the varnishing is done should have a temperature of between 75 and 80 degrees.

3. Follow manufacturer's direction as to time of drying. When thoroughly dry, sand lightly with No. 4/0 sandpaper, because varnish does not adhere to a glossy surface. Apply one or two coats more.

RUBBING A VARNISHED SURFACE.—1. Varnish is rubbed to a smooth surface with a felt pad and powdered pumice stone. The felt may be glued to a piece of wood.

2. Dip the pad in a paraffin oil or other mineral oil, and also pour a little oil on the surface. Sprinkle No. FF pumice stone on the surface and rub with the grain (Fig. 67). Take an extra short stroke at each end to overcome the tendency to rub too much in the middle.

3. Proceed cautiously and clean off the surface frequently to inspect it.

4. When the surface is perfectly smooth, it may be given a higher gloss if the rubbing is continued with powdered rotten stone, which is finer than pumice stone.

5. If a higher polish is desired, the procedure is the same except that water is used as a lubricant instead of oil. After rubbing with the rotten stone, the surface is cleaned off with a chamois skin and rubbed with a polishing oil. A linen rag or a piece of cheesecloth moistened with the polish is used. Rub briskly until the whole surface has a high gloss.

6. The excess oil is cleaned off with a pad made of a linen rag wrapped around a piece of cotton waste. Moisten the waste with a little alcohol, fold the linen over it and rub the surface lightly and briskly. Never let the pad rest for a fraction of a second, as the alcohol otherwise will burn through the varnish.

FIG. 67—Rubbing varnished surface with powdered pumice stone and water

Lacquer may be used for producing a polish instead of varnish.

1. If lacquer is used, an undercoating of thin shellac should always be given. This is particularly important if paste wood filler has been used, because lacquer dissolves the filler.

2. Two or three coats of lacquer should be given. No sanding is necessary between coats. Spraying lacquer must be sprayed on; brushing lacquer should be put on very thick with a soft brush and the work should be done quickly because the lacquer dries very fast.

3. Lacquer is rubbed with 400A Wet-or-Dry silicon carbide paper and oil. It is more difficult to rub without going through the finish than varnish. Great care must therefore be taken, and the surface inspected frequently.

4. When the rubbing is completed, the surface is cleaned and given a high polish with a special rubbing and polishing compound. It is rubbed on with a rag or a piece of waste and no special precautions are necessary.

91

SUGGESTED PROJECTS

FOR the first veneering job it is recommended not to attempt anything too difficult and elaborate, but rather to make a small piece of furniture, such as the projects* now to be described. It is at once apparent how the judicious use of veneer enhances their beauty and charm and lifts them above the commonplace.

Besides the pleasure and satisfaction that come to one through the planning and execution of such fascinating work, it also pays dividends. Anyone can easily find this out for himself by deducting the small cost of the materials entering into the construction of such articles of furniture from the price that similar pieces sell for in the stores.

The Book-Rack illustrated in Fig. 68 is of the type that can be extended. It has the added advantage that it can be packed flat because the ends are hinged to the bottom.

1. The bottom consists of one central board, $4\frac{1}{2}''$ wide, which slides between two strips $1''$ wide. These three pieces are all $\frac{3}{4}''$ thick and $16\frac{1}{2}''$ long. Cut and plane them to dimensions.

2. Then cut the tongues and grooves as shown in the cross-section. This is best done on a small circular saw, but may also be done by hand with a match plane.

3. Saw $3''$ off each of the three pieces. Glue the wide piece between the two narrow ones, $13\frac{1}{2}''$ long, so that their ends are flush, and glue the two $3''$ narrow pieces on each side of the $4\frac{1}{2}''$ x $13\frac{1}{2}''$ piece.

4. A small cleat $\frac{1}{4}''$ x $\frac{1}{2}''$ x $3\frac{3}{4}''$ is screwed to the underside of the middle piece and a $5/16''$ x $1''$ x $6\frac{1}{2}''$ cleat is screwed to the two narrow outside pieces. These cleats act as stops for the sliding mechanism. This book-rack is designed to extend $24''$.

5. The ends may be shaped and veneered in a number of different ways. The design suggested consists of a central panel of figured veneer,

---

* Complete materials for making the five projects described in this chapter (except the core stock) are included in the Constantine Home Course of Instruction in Veneering.

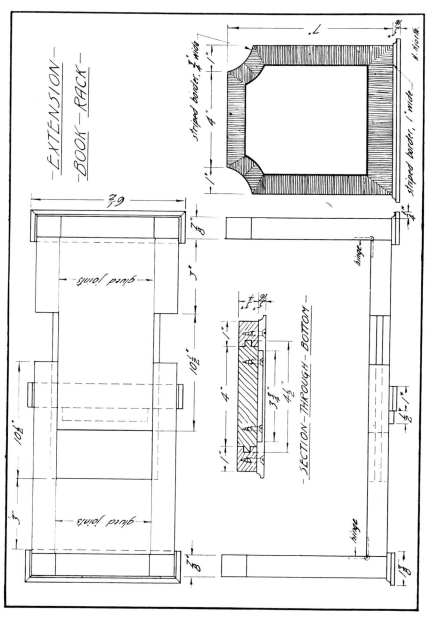

FIG. 68—Extension book-rack

as, for example, mahogany, a 1/16″ black line and a border of a striped wood, such as zebrawood or East Indian rosewood.

6. It is recommended to lay out the design on the ends, shape the central panel and fasten it with veneer pins, two of which should be marked for re-locating the panel when gluing. The black line is now fitted around it. The curved part may easily be bent to shape by moistening it with a little hot water. The border is glued up in long strips as explained on page 60, jointed and mitered, after which it is tacked in place and taped. The small curves on the panel and border may be cut with a pair of dividers, one leg of which has been sharpened to a knife point.

7. No crossbands are needed on this small job if the wood is well seasoned, but the inside faces of the ends should be veneered with plain figured veneer.

8. After trimming and sanding the veneer, the ends are hinged to the bottom. The two cleats are then made and screwed to the ends. A piece of felt may be glued to these cleats, as well as to that in the center, in order to protect the surface of the table top on which the finished book-rack may be placed.

The Mirror Frame (Fig. 69) is a very interesting and useful project. The processes of construction are as follows:

1. The frame consists of four pieces joined with mortise and tenon joints as shown in the detail on the drawing. Before these pieces are joined together the rabbets for the mirror must be cut. Note that they stop at the mortises on the vertical pieces.

2. After the frame has been glued, the top piece is made and fitted with dowels to its upper edge. The whole frame is then smoothed and the top piece removed. The frame is now veneered as suggested. The veneer may either be striped or figured, cut across the grain, as shown, or along the grain. Lay out the miters on the frame, cut and joint the veneer to fit these, and tape them together. They should project about 1/4″ over all edges of the frame.

3. When gluing the veneer to the frame, it is well to cut cleats of wood to fit into the rabbets so that the pressure will be evenly distributed. Trim the edges of the veneer after gluing, remove the tape and sand smooth. The 3/16″ molding is now made and glued around the inside edges of the frame.

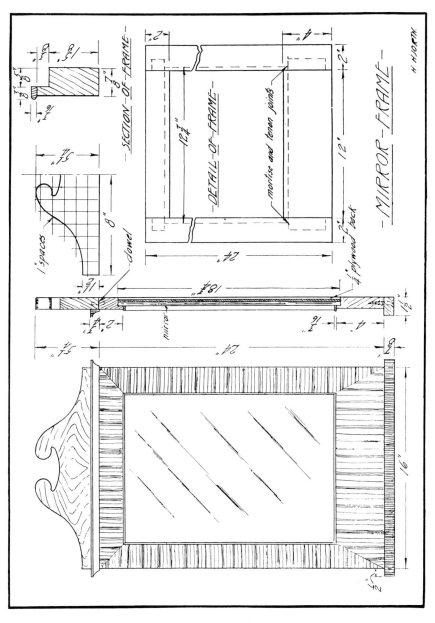

FIG. 69—Mirror frame

95

4. Two pieces of highly figured wood such as crotch mahogany joined end to end are suggested for the top piece.

5. After gluing, trimming, and sanding, the top piece is glued permanently to the frame. The joint is covered with a piece of molding glued over it and carried around the sides.

6. The bottom of the frame is finished with a $\frac{7}{8}''$ x $1\frac{1}{2}''$ strip screwed to it. This strip may be veneered on the edges, as shown in the drawing.

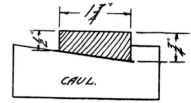

FIG. 70—Veneering picture frame moulding

7. The mirror, which is $12\frac{5}{8}''$ x $18\frac{5}{8}''$, should be of $\frac{1}{4}''$ plate glass. Place a piece of paper over its back and then nail a backing made of $\frac{1}{4}''$ plywood to the rabbet. Glue a piece of paper over the rabbets and back to keep out the dust.

Picture Frames can be made by preparing and veneering the molding in suitable lengths, after which the rabbets are cut and the molding mitered in the usual way. Fig. 70 shows how a beveled molding is veneered. The moldings should all be sawed at the same time on a circular saw tilted to the desired angle. It follows that the caul board should also be cut at this angle.

A Serving Tray, such as illustrated in Fig. 71, is one of the most useful pieces of furniture around the home.

1. The bottom of the tray is best made from a piece of $\frac{1}{4}''$ plywood or a piece of hard fibreboard of the same thickness. The veneer design suggested is the diamond pattern which is described on page 55. Four-piece matching of highly figured wood such as burl walnut or crotch mahogany is also suitable, but more difficult to lay. If the bottom is made from solid wood, crossbanding is essential before laying the face veneers. If plywood or hard fibreboard is used, the crossbanding may be omitted.

2. The molding is built up of three pieces, as shown in the detail on the drawing. The central piece is veneered as the picture frame molding, shown in Fig. 70, and the two other pieces are shaped with a scratch stock (Fig. 62). These three pieces are then glued together,

96

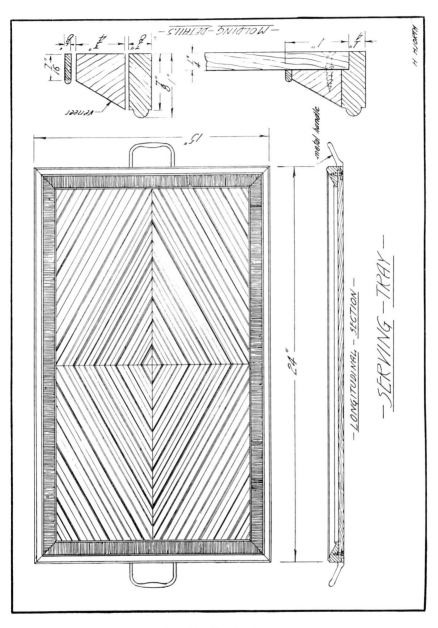

FIG. 71—Serving tray

97

FIG. 72—Coffee table

after which the rabbet is cut and the molding mitered and glued in the corners.

3. The bottom is fastened to the molding with screws.

4. Two brass handles are set in flush with the bottom and fastened to it with screws.

The Coffee Table (Figs. 72 and 73) goes well with the serving tray and is also a very desirable and popular piece of furniture.

1. A template is first made of the legs which are sawed from $1\frac{1}{2}''$ stock. They are then smoothed and tapered on the two flat sides.

2. The top is then made from several narrow pieces of wood glued together. It should be made of the same kind of wood as the rest of the table. See description of making a core, page 46, and Fig. 3.

3. After planing and smoothing, the top is cut round and veneered with crossbanding on both sides.

4. The position of the four legs and circular rail are now marked out on one side of the top, and a template made of one section of the rail.

5. The rails may be sawed from a $2\frac{1}{2}''$ solid plank or from a piece built up of several boards glued together. They may easily be sanded smooth on a sanding disk.

6. After sanding, the rails are cut and fitted according to the layout on the top. They are doweled together with the legs. If the rails are cut from built-up wood, they should be veneered (Fig. 55).

7. The stretchers are joined in the middle with a cross-lap joint and mortised into the legs.

8. The table is now ready for gluing. The stretchers are clamped to the legs with bar clamps, while the joints between the circular rails and legs are brought together by twisting two strands of rope. If the rails

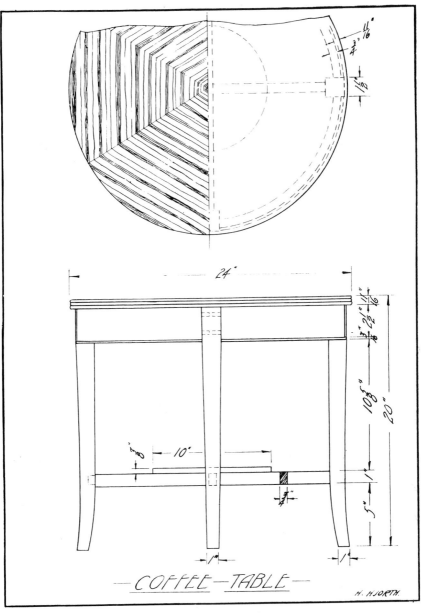

COFFEE-TABLE

FIG. 73—Coffee table

99

are veneered, particular care must be taken to protect them from the rope biting into them when it is being twisted.

9. The face veneers are then matched and glued (see description on page 61), after which the edge is shaped with a scratch stock (Fig. 62).

10. The top is fastened to the rails with 3″ x 12 screws passing through the rails. The underside of the rails may be finished with a 3/16″ molding as shown.

11. The small 10″ shelf may be made from $\frac{3}{8}$″ plywood and veneered on its face only. It is fastened with $1\frac{1}{4}$″ x 10 screws to the stretchers.

12. The table is finally given a thorough sanding and inspection before the finish is applied.

The Jewel Box (Fig. 74) is an interesting little project requiring some care and patience in execution. By changing the dimensions, the box may serve for other purposes, such as a sewing box or a humidor.

1. The ends of the box are fitted into the sides with a dado and rabbet joint, after which the top and bottom are glued in place.

2. After smoothing the surface the box is veneered across the grain on all surfaces (crossbanding). This is especially necessary on the ends, where the endwood otherwise is liable to show through the face veneers.

3. The panels on the top, sides and ends are now made. The line and inset on the top are inlaid after the veneer is glued in place. The top veneer is therefore made up only of a figured panel surrounded by a striped border. Lay out the design on the box, cut the figured panel to approximate size, tack in place and trim the edges with a very sharp knife. Prepare the border as explained on page 60, miter the corners and tape together. Always mark two or more veneer pins for re-location of the panel.

4. Prepare the other panels in the same way and glue on two opposite surfaces at a time.

5. After all the surfaces have been veneered the $\frac{1}{8}$″ x $\frac{1}{8}$″ black line is inlaid on the edge around the top as explained on page 82. The other lines and the inset in the top are then inlaid.

6. The box is now given a careful sanding, after which it is cut through all around, $1\frac{1}{4}$″ from the top.

7. After hinging the lid and inserting the lock, the box is ready for finishing.

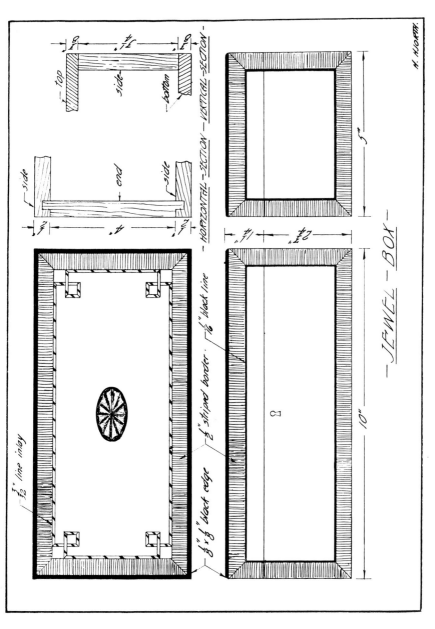

FIG. 74—Jewel Box

101

ACCOMPLISHMENTS OF MODERN-DAY CRAFTSMEN

When the requirements of one's home have been satisfied by the amateur furniture builder, where can he turn for further endeavor? To the limitless field of veneering! The creative mind and the skillful, practiced hands of the craftsmen will never stop for want of what to make. Veneering, when combined with inlaying, offers the widest conceivable variety of craftwork, as attested by the many fine examples of projects which have been accomplished by clerks and bankers, teachers and preachers, school boys and elderly men. Veneering is the hobby that satisfies them all!

VENEERED BOX
with border and emblem inlays, by Charles Burgess of New York City

JEWEL BOX. In this example of fine craftsmanship Theodore Cichy of Philadelphia proves that inlays can be as delicate as metal chasing

CHECKERTOP. For checkers or chess, this perennial favorite project was completed by Frank S. Wystrach, Chicago

INLAID TABLE Creative talents find expression in this modern design inlaid in the hexagonal top of table by W. M. Dunham, Rochester, Pa.

GRANDFATHER'S CLOCK. This seventy-three inch "tall clock" made by Captain Victor Goudey of Middletown, Pa., illustrates how the simple introduction of fine inlay lines in base and waist add just the right emphasis to the vertical-grain mahogany

VIOLIN. Veneering the curved panels for violins was accomplished by a man with one arm, Leonard Porter of Kansas City, Mo.

THEATER Puppetry takes a new dimension in this animated theater cabinet made by Olan J. Cooper, Chico, Calif. It is an elaborate example of the inlaying art. Contains 85 woods and veneers; stands over 7 feet high; has 18 actors 10 inches high

INLAID PICTURE. Norman L. Maile of London, inlaid this 16th-century house scene by skillfully combining walnut, ebony and sycamore veneers

PEMBROKE TABLE. Simple beauty in the basic design favors veneers in rich colors and pronounced grain, as chosen by Dard Hunter, Jr., Chillicothe, Ohio when he applied crotch mahogany and striped satinwood

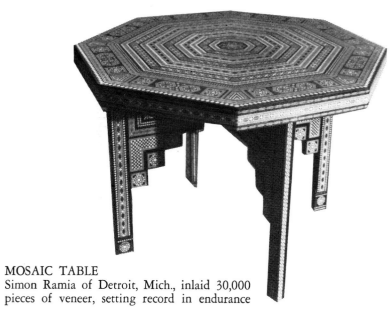

MOSAIC TABLE
Simon Ramia of Detroit, Mich., inlaid 30,000 pieces of veneer, setting record in endurance

HARPSICHORD. Example of good judgment in choosing a veneer-faced panel for lid, to resist warp. Howard Everngam

CREDENZA. Fifteen-drawer curved-front chest shows how Texan Chris H. Groneman skillfully matched myrtle

BOW-FRONT CABINET. The curved panels and doors of this fine credenza required curved forms for laminating layers of veneer. Anthony Bosco of Everett, Mass., builder of the piece, combined mahogany crotch veneer with contrasting tulipwood borders

COFFEE TABLE. In modern construction large plain areas would be uninteresting without the decorative value of rich-looking veneer. Coffee table by Charles Quantz, Oakland, Cal. utilizes pleasing striped walnut

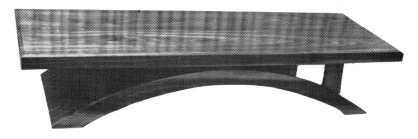

VENEERING WITHOUT CLAMPS

E ven in this age when scientific men are announcing almost daily their achievements of the impossible, it has not occurred to the woodworker to watch for miracles in his field. He is not accustomed to major developments in tools and techniques. Woodworking has been practiced in about the same way for centuries. True, power tools came along in the last half of the 19th century and speeded things up, but the furniture they produce is a doubtful improvement over hand work.

In veneering, too, essentially the same methods have prevailed for centuries. When a revolutionary advance in veneering methods finally comes along, as now, it deserves dramatic emphasis.

To dramatize adhesive quality of new glue, veneer was applied to sharply curved metal surface. In this case, an empty bean can

To point up the new possibilities in veneering, a common, empty bean can was covered with thin wood veneer. The wood was attached with liquid adhesive to a rounded metal surface of short radius, and no clamps were used. This tough assignment for the adhesive was purposeful. If a bean can could be veneered without clamps, almost anything else could be easily veneered.

The wood veneer chosen to convert the can into a vase had no new qualities. The metal surface of the bean can was stubbornly resistive to adhesive as always. But the adhesive employed in this demonstration was new. It possessed the remarkable characteristic of welding instantly on contact, without sustained pressure. In other words, here was an adhesive so strong that it eliminated the need for clamping.

The adhesive used in the demonstration had been developed especially for veneering, and had undergone extensive trial before it was marketed as Constantine's Veneer Glue. It now is being used widely by cabinetmakers, furniture manufacturers and other professional woodworkers. In containers of pint, quart and gallon sizes it also has been made available for home and school workshops.

The development of Veneer Glue introduced a completely new technique. It opened the way toward new craftwork adventure and new woodworking accomplishments. Where previously it was not practicable to apply enriching veneers to various surfaces, now almost any craftwork creation, nearly any piece of furniture or any home accessory of wood or metal can be improved in appearance by covering it with colorful, figured veneer.

Veneering over old surfaces — such as existing furniture pieces — could heretofore be accomplished only in very limited places. You cannot take a piece of furniture apart to clamp on a veneer face. Refinishing was the difficult alternative. But now it is a relatively simple job to recondition by covering an old surface with veneer in an exciting new color and figure. This area of woodworking offers unlimited possibilities both around one's own home and in the way of part-time, profitable work.

In renovating, the opportunities are numerous. Dressers, chests, and cabinets become scarred. Table tops — dining tables and coffee tables principally — acquire stains and scratches that are beyond touchup refinishing. Any of these pieces in almost every home is a prospect for veneering, now that the work can be done in the kitchen, or if necessary, where the piece stands. When faced with new veneer and finished with any of the simpler, modern finishing materials, the old piece takes on a value far exceeding effort and expense.

More obvious opportunities in veneering, by the simpler method of using Veneer Glue and no clamps, occur in original craft projects. Anyone who likes woodworking as a hobby will readily see innumerable ways to utilize the new procedure. Cheaper woods may be used for foundation construction — table tops, chest sides, drawer fronts and so on. These woods can be covered at relatively low cost with exotic woods in the form of veneer. The dollar saving is substantial; and the finished piece looks expensively elegant. Inlay picture making, and use of inlay borders and designs, also are made easier by the new veneering method.

Although veneering without clamps is so simple as to require no practice, a brief study of techniques and handling of materials is recommended. Once understood, the rules are easily remembered. Veneering, plain and fancy, without special equipment now becomes an adventure not to be delayed.

GENERAL PROCEDURE. The following instructions apply to the

Recovering large cabinet with interesting face veneer is
accomplished without clamps. New gluing method is used

new, easy way of bonding veneer to another surface. Depending on
the project, the veneer you are using may be wide enough so that no
joints are required. In this case, merely cut the veneer approximately
to size, allowing a little extra all around. The overhang will be trimmed
off after the veneer has been bonded in place. If a joint is necessary
in the veneer or you are making up a so-called matched face, trim the
joining edges very accurately and fasten them temporarily together
with regular veneer tape or any self-adhering tape, applied to the face
side. Taping is described in detail on page 53.

If you are working with an inlaid picture or other marquetry face
it should be treated as a single sheet of veneer, the face surface being
covered in the usual way with paper or strips of tape. Detailed instructions on preparing the veneer sheet are contained in the Constantine
"Wood Pix Manual." The procedure is the same up to this point
whether you use the new Constantine Veneer Glue or whether you
use one of the older types of glues requiring cauls, forms, clamps, or
veneer presses.

In using the new Veneer Glue sand lightly, if necessary, the side of
the veneer which is to be glued down. It must be perfectly clean and
smooth. See that the panel core, hardboard or wood surface to which

110

the veneer is to be bonded also is smooth, flat, free from grease, wax or oil and in good condition. If you are veneering a surface that has already been varnished, painted or otherwise finished, it is desirable to remove the old finish with varnish remover and then sand the surface lightly. However, if the old finish is in good condition, removal is not essential.

If the surface on which you are applying the veneer has been glued up from several pieces or has noticeable defects, or if there is any danger of cracking in time, cover it first with what we call crossbanding; that is, some plain, inexpensive veneer such as poplar. Crossbanding should be laid so that the grain runs at right angles to the grain of the face veneer which will later cover it. Veneer Glue may be used for applying the crossbanding in exactly the same way as the face veneer, but crossbanding and facing should be handled as two separate operations.

GLUING. Thoroughly stir the veneer glue. Applying the glue is a quick, simple operation, but to insure best results it will be described in detail. While you have to wait for several coats to dry before making the bond, you really gain time over ordinary gluing methods because you do not work with clamps or a veneer press, and there is no waiting time afterwards while the glue hardens. For most veneering purposes it is best to apply Veneer Glue with an inexpensive but clean brush. Don't brush back and forth; instead, flow the glue on in a smooth, uniform coat. Use plenty of glue. Be sure it covers the surface completely, but don't let it pile up more thickly in some spots than others. Use equal care in applying the glue to the veneer and to the surface to which the veneer is to be cemented. Now let the glue dry while you turn your attention to other work. Drying will take 30 minutes or longer. Don't try to hurry the process; in fact it is a good idea to wait for an hour.

The next step is to apply a second coat of glue to the surface on which the veneer is to be glued and to the veneer itself. This is done in exactly the same way as previously. Let it dry 30 minutes or more. The third step is to inspect the surfaces. The pores of the wood should be well filled. The surfaces should have a uniformly glossy look, almost as if they had been varnished. Look at them from side to side to be sure there are no dull spots. Certain woods are quite porous and absorb more glue than others, so don't be surprised if you find a third coat of glue is needed. Apply it as before and again wait until it is thoroughly dry — at least 30 minutes, although it can wait as long as two hours.

READY TEST. If you want to be sure that the glue is entirely dry, ready for bonding, there is a simple test. Take a scrap of wrapping paper and press it against the glue-coated surface. Remove the paper and see if any glue has adhered to it. If not, the glue is dry enough for bonding. However, one should not wait too long. An hour is an ideal time. If you have waited too long because of an unavoidable interruption, all you have to do is to apply another coat of glue before making the bond and let it dry approximately 30 minutes.

PERFECT ALIGNMENT. Making the bond is simplicity itself, except for one thing. The glue grips instantly when you place two glued surfaces in contact. You can't slide or shift the work around. If, therefore, you are gluing down an inlaid picture or other marquetry work, a matched face, or a piece of veneer that is barely large enough to cover the surface to which it is being applied, you have to be sure to locate it properly.

SLIPSHEET SEPARATOR. Exact alignment is much easier to achieve than you might think. Cut a sheet of wrapping paper as large as the surface being veneered. Place it on the glued surface and lay the veneer, glue side down, over it. The paper separates the glued surfaces but does not itself adhere to either. Now align the surface and veneer perfectly. Keeping them in place, take hold of the bottom edge of the sheet of paper and withdraw it about two inches. Now, being sure that the veneer is still perfectly aligned, press it down along the top edge where there is no longer any paper between the two glued surfaces. Then you can withdraw entirely the paper, or "slipsheet" as it is called. We cannot emphasize this point too much. It is a little trick that is not universally known. You must remember that you have no second choice. THE INSTANT TWO COATED SURFACES TOUCH EACH OTHER, A BOND IS FORMED WHICH CANNOT BE CHANGED.

Now press the veneer down firmly. The simplest way usually is to use a rubber roller. A small one is adequate for most work, but where large surfaces are involved, or even where small surfaces are worked, a clean rolling pin may well be employed. If no roller is available, the veneer may be tapped down all over with a rubber mallet, or a small softwood block can be tapped lightly with a hammer against the veneer surface. This last mentioned method is especially convenient when veneering relatively narrow edges. Be sure not to miss any spots in rolling or tapping, or blisters may develop in the veneer.

This completes the gluing operation. It is as simple as that, and now there is no waiting time or overnight, or a day, or two days for the glue to harden. You may trim any projecting edges of veneer or do what other work has to be done in this connection, and proceed immediately with the type of finish you have selected.

In this connection, several aids are available. The "Constantine Wood Finishing Manual" for 25¢ is recommended. The Course in Professional Wood Finishing as given in the New York headquarters of Albert Constantine and Son offers excellent practical instruction. A complete transcript of the course, available postpaid by mail, costs $3.00 per copy. The foregoing instructions given for gluing wood to wood apply also when bonding wood to metal. With this glue, veneers may be bonded to a metal surface as well as to a wood surface. To take a practical example, suppose you have a kitchen where all the cabinets are in birch or some other wood but, as often is the case, you have a dishwasher with an enameled or stainless steel front and you would like to have the front of the dishwasher match the rest of the cabinets. It is very easy to apply matching birch veneer with the aid of Constantine's Veneer Glue.

TEMPERATURE REQUIREMENTS. In gluing, the temperature of the room must be 70 degrees Fahrenheit or warmer, and the wood and glue should also be at room temperature. If your shop cannot be brought up to 70 degrees in winter, work in the kitchen or another room. Gluing is now a comparatively clean operation. Spread out a few newspapers and do the work wherever it is warm enough.

After applying the glue, clean the brush with lacquer thinner. For covering large horizontal areas as kitchen counters or table tops, a notched metal applicator may be used for spreading the glue. This tool spreads the glue quickly and uniformly.

IMPROPER ADHESION. If, after bonding the veneer, you discover it is not adhering properly, you either did not apply sufficient glue to satisfy the unusual porosity of the veneer you are using, or you let the glue dry too long, or you failed to roll or tap down the veneer sufficiently over the entire surface. Sometimes in such cases, if you discover the defect within a day or two, you can reactivate the glue by applying moderate heat with an ordinary electric lamp, a heat lamp or an electric iron. Simply warm the area and roll or tap down the veneer.

NON-STAINING. One of the great advantages of Veneer Glue is that it does not stain. It resists moisture and water as well as most chemicals. Within certain limits it gets stronger with age. Its strength is more than ample for veneering, but it is not intended to be used as a joint glue in cabinetmaking.

BALANCED CONSTRUCTION IN VENEERING. One of the remarkable modifications in standard veneering practice has been made possible by the development of Veneer Glue. Every previous text on veneering stresses the importance of what is called "balanced construction" in veneering. Veneer and plywood plants go to immense trouble and ex-

113

pense to design cores which resist warping when veneer is applied.

The general rule is that a built-up panel used as a free-standing member such as a flush door, the drop leaf of a table, an inlay picture plaque, gameboard or tray, should have the same number of sheets of veneers, and approximately the same type and thickness, on each side to reduce the likelihood of warping.

Many experiments conducted recently with the new Constantine's Veneer Glue show no need for a backing veneer in many cases where it would have been essential with previous methods of veneering. Where it is not necessary to veneer the reverse side, the advantages would be considerable as far as the amateur craftsman is concerned.

In the experiments we chose an extreme example of a panel of un-balanced construction. We used a redwood core about $\frac{1}{8}''$ thick. This core was veneered on one side only with mahogany crossbanding and mahogany face veneer. To emphasize this unbalanced construction, eight heavy coats of glue were used, two being applied to one side of the core, two to one side of the crossbanding; then two to the other side of the crossbanding, and two to the face veneer. One could not picture a more unbalanced assembly than this, and with almost any other type of adhesive this panel would have shown a severe curve within a day after coming out of the press. But our test panel remained straight.

The reason for this absence of warp is that the new type of adhesive is a rubber-based adhesive and presumably does not cause either the core or the veneer to absorb moisture. The normal type of water-mixed glue causes the veneer to expand. The expansion is considerable. That is why ordinary glues are never spread on the veneer itself but on the panel or core, and that is the reason pressure is applied as quickly as possible after the veneers have been laid. Under pressure the veneer will have little opportunity to absorb moisture from the glue and ex-pand. Even so, there is a tendency for the veneer to shrink as the glue dries. In some cases if the pressure is sufficient to prevent the veneer from shrinking, the veneer will split.

While the characteristic of Veneer Glue which permits unbalanced construction without warpage may not be the most dramatic point to remember, it comes very close to being the most important. Ranking ahead of it, in the gratitude of the amateur woodworker, undoubtedly will be the ability of the new Veneer Glue to weld veneers instantly without clamps or sustained pressure, thus greatly extending the scope of veneering.

APPENDIX

W HERE to obtain veneers, crossbanding, core stock, inlays, borders and other essentials for veneering in retail quantities is not widely known among amateur woodworkers. This is one reason why more craftsmen, small woodworking shops and school workshops have not taken advantage of the veneering process.

Practically all materials mentioned in this book may be obtained from the publisher. *Constantine's Manual for Craftsmen,* which is a standard reference work on this subject, contains a large full-color identification chart of veneers and cabinet woods.

The veneers listed in Chapter IV are available in quantities of three square feet or more, and are supplied in commercial quantities to furniture and piano manufacturers and other large users.

A complete course in veneering, prepared by Mr. Hjorth and based on the projects in this book, may be obtained in a single economical package. There is sufficient veneer, crossbanding and other materials for veneering all five projects—selected mahogany veneers, striped walnut, striped East Indian rosewood, cedar or mahogany crotch veneer, mottled and striped satinwood veneer, borders, glue and glue brush, veneer pins and tape, and a veneer saw.

Pre-cut inlaid picture kits are supplied as another aid to beginners. These have

Complete veneering course

the veneer for the elements of each picture carefully jigsawed to shape by professional marquetry cutters so that they can be assembled very easily by anyone without tools or clamps. These kits make a good introduction to veneering because they embody the basic principles and,

Map of U.S. and Guiding Star show
two popular pre-cut kit subjects

indeed, represent one of the best ways to interest a beginner in the fascinating art of veneering. Pre-cut kits provide an easy beginning in handling, assembling and gluing veneers; and they offer a generous reward in a finished all-wood picture. Pre-cut kits developed by Constantine include all parts pre-cut, ready for assembly. There is no cutting to do, and no clamping required. In addition to the veneers, all borders, backing panel, full-size patterns, sandpaper, adhesive and complete instructions are included. Pre-cut kits vary in size and complexity. One group measures 12″ x 15½″. Subjects in this range include Mountain Stream, Flying Ducks, Old Mill, Yachting in Summer. These pictures, and larger sizes, make impressive wall pictures. Sizes measuring 16″ wide up to 22″ include American Emblem, Tigers at Dusk, Pheasant Family, Colonial Tavern, Father Time Clock, Cocker Spaniel. These and many others often serve as end-table tops or serving trays. Assembly is accomplished anywhere, even on a cardtable while watching TV.

Glues are most important, as was made clear in Chapter V. There a few typical glues were mentioned by name, but a more complete list will now be given for this reason: the trade names of glues often do not reveal the type or classification to which they belong.

Urea resin glue: Cascamite, Formica Urea Resin, LePage's Plastic Resin, National Casein's DR-2 and Weldwood. *Liquid hide glue:* Franklin. *Liquid fish glue:* LePage's, Rogers. *Casein glue:* Casco, Formica Casein Glue, LePage's Casein Glue, National Casein's Casein Glue, *Resorcinol resin glue:* Elmer's Waterproof Glue (Cascophen), National Casein's R-3, U. S. Plywood Phenol Resorcinol Glue. *White polyvinyl liquid glue:* Elmer's Glue-All (Cascorez), Evertite Liquid Resin Glue, LePage's Sure Grip White Glue, National Casein's 5000 and 5900, Weldwood Presto-Set Glue. *Cements containing rubber:* Constantine's Veneer Glue, Casco Flexible Cement, Formica Contact Bond Cement, Pliobond, Weldwood Contact Cement.

Marquetry picture kits. A more advanced form of wood picture making, called marquetry, is perhaps the highest artistic development in veneering. Marquetry kits offered by Constantine contain a wide range of colorful veneers to be cut to shape with a sharp knife and the parts assembled on a full-size pattern provided with other materials in the kit. The unique Constantine method permits including fine details or omitting some details so each craftsman can work at his own level of skill. Kit subjects include Florida Everglades, Owl, Roses, World Beneath the Sea. Many others.

Lucky Strike marquetry

Fraternal emblems composed of beautiful rare woods, inlaid to form an assembled veneer face 1/28″ in thickness, have now been made available for craftwork. Each emblem, composed of various kinds of exotic woods selected for color value, measures 8″ in diameter and is set in a 12″ square of beautiful American walnut. These emblems represent unusually fine examples of marquetry work. Individual pieces have been sawed and fitted with infinite skill by professional inlayers.

In addition to the apparent purpose as wall plaques when mounted on ¼″ hardboard backing, the unmounted emblems are suited to use as decorative inlays in card-table tops, desk tops, chests, cabinets, serving trays and other furniture surfaces. They can be inset as supplied

Rarewood veneers used in inlaid fraternal emblems

117

with the framing square of walnut, or the circular emblem can be removed from the square and used alone.

The Constantine company, originators of these emblems for craftwork, offers eight popular designs: Eastern Star, Knights of Columbus, Shriners, Masonic, Lions, Elks, Rotary and Kiwanis.

The complete story of woods, including a full listing and description of all types of veneers, many more than are discussed in *Veneering Made Easy,* has been brought together in a single volume entitled *Know Your Woods.* This is an exciting account, by Albert Constantine, Jr., of all the things you want to know about the woods you use and the woods you have never heard of. One of the country's best-known authorities on woods of the world, Mr. Constantine has included facts and photographs from his personal collection to make this book of special value to woodworker, collector, student and teacher.

Know Your Woods book gives the common, scientific and locality names for woods. Over 1,400 woods are indexed. More than 80 special close-up photos of wood grain, 256 instructive drawings and several hundred additional photos supply all the visual aids available for identification of trees and the woods they produce. Published at $5.75, this book is highly recommended for its factual content with answers to all questions about wood, and equally for lifting the story of woods into the realm of fascinating reading.

INDEX